Swan

D1536515

Animal
Series editor: Jonathan Burt

Already published

Crow
Boria Sax

Ant
Charlotte Sleigh

Tortoise
Peter Young

Cockroach
Marion Copeland

Dog
Susan McHugh

Oyster
Rebecca Stott

Bear
Robert E. Bieder

Bee
Claire Preston

Rat
Jonathan Burt

Snake
Drake Stutesman

Falcon
Helen Macdonald

Whale
Joe Roman

Parrot
Paul Carter

Tiger
Susie Green

Salmon
Peter Coates

Fox
Martin Wallen

Fly
Steven Connor

Cat
Katharine M. Rogers

Peacock
Christine E. Jackson

Cow
Hannah Velten

Duck
Victoria de Rijke

Shark
Dean Crawford

Forthcoming

Moose
Kevin Jackson

Hare
Simon Carnell

Spider
Katja and Sergiusz Michalski

Pig
Brett Mizelle

Worm
Daniel Brass

Rhinoceros
Kelly Enright

Pigeon
Barbara Allen

Camel
Robert Irwin

Chicken
Annie Potts

Wolf
Garry Marvin

Horse
Elaine Walker

Penguin
Stephen Martin

Elephant
Daniel Wylie

Ape
John Sorenson

Butterfly
Matthew Brower

Sheep
Philip Armstrong

Swan

Peter Young

REAKTION BOOKS

Published by
REAKTION BOOKS LTD
33 Great Sutton Street
London EC1V 0DX, UK
www.reaktionbooks.co.uk

First published 2008

Printed and bound in China

British Library Cataloguing in Publication Data
Young, Peter
    Swan. – (Animal)
    1. Swans 2. Animals and civilization
    I. Title
    598.4'18

    ISBN–13: 978 1 86189 349 9

Contents

Introduction

Swans have all the elegance and freshness of youth. Their anatomical structure gives them a majesty and grace, whether in formation flight or cruising effortlessly on a lake. In particular the distinctive curve of the neck has been praised by poets and copied by designers, especially in an age of elegance like the eighteenth century. Swans are a natural subject for the creative arts: architecture, ballet, décor, music, painting and sculpture. Classical myths such as Leda and the swan have had an artistic appeal enduring to the present. Astronomers have seen its form in a constellation. When Thomas Young observed the intersecting ripples swans created on a Cambridge college lake they set him thinking on the nature of light, which he saw as a wave. His theory was a radical departure from Newton's view that light was a series of particles. Pasteur used swan-necked flasks to demonstrate a germ theory of disease. It was a major advance in bacteriology, replacing the notion of the spontaneous generation of disease.

Until 1697, when the existence of black swans in Australia was made known to the western world, it was believed that all swans were white. Their image was of purity, enlightenment, innocence and virginity. Reappraising them took time. It also increased doubts about propositions based on inductive logic. How valid is it to reason from the particular to the general? How strong is 'proof' and are some sciences only pseudo sciences?

Much lore associated with swans has a common theme: transformation. This is much more than simply changing from an ugly duckling into a beautiful swan, as in Hans Christian Andersen's fairy story mirroring his own life. Tales of transformation from bird to human form and back again, often in the nick of time, are believed to have originated in the Orient and are found in Graeco-Roman, Celtic, Norse, Teutonic and Native American cultures.

Occurring frequently in folklore is the story of the swan-maiden who has the ability to switch between the two identities, her bird form represented by a feathered cloak. Man can achieve dominance over her by stealing and hiding her cloak, but there usually comes a time when she can retrieve it and, to his distress, fly away into her natural environment. Her male counterpart is the swan-knight, Lohengrin.

What these legends emphasize is the dual nature of swans. The general reflection, like the bird itself on calm water, is of grace with quiet power, which nevertheless does not prevent it from becoming the victim of vandals. An outstanding beauty of the bird kingdom, it is also a symbol of quality attached to many products and services. In practice swans are not all sweetness and light. They can be vicious fighters, not just in defence of nests and cygnets. In-fighting between species occurs and perceived enemies, apparently stronger, are killed. They are not necessarily faithful to partners for life.

The dichotomy is seen in conservation. For instance, in North America the trumpeter swan was hunted for food, feathers and skins almost to extinction. Today, following sustained pressure from concerned voluntary bodies, the species flourishes again. Yet there are those who question whether conservation is not going too far, leading to overpopulation. Anglers argue that too many swans can strip the plant life of rivers to the detriment of fish and hence their sport. For some they are 'feathered missiles' presenting a threat to expanding aviation.

Perhaps the greatest potential danger though is in the transmission of disease. Spring and autumn migrations involve long distances and swans can be continental carriers of the bird flu virus. Reputedly singing before their own death, they could be responsible for a pandemic affecting millions of people.

1 Clamorous Wings

Of more than 8,000 species of birds, the swan is surely one of the most readily recognized. With its long slender neck, it glides gracefully, serenely on water. Its large webbed feet and short legs, awkward on land, propel it effortlessly in its natural element. A curved neck imparts majesty; a straight neck gives it a haughty air. Ornamenting lakes and rivers, it is a scene-stealer. In Britain, where it is a protected bird, it is justly described as the royalty of wildfowl.

Its beauty is a result of long evolution. Recent DNA analysis has shown that the native British mute swan is more closely related than other species to its prehistoric ancestors, which evolved ultimately from dinosaurs. Accordingly, since 2002 the mute swan, hitherto classified on its anatomical structure, has headed the British list of bird species, replacing another waterfowl, the red-throated diver.[1]

Airborne, the swan is a majestic sight. With slow wing beats and an outstretched neck, it flies elegantly and strongly to a determined destination. It is the fastest waterfowl on water or in the air. Flying in diagonal or v-formation, a mass of hundreds of swans is a wildlife spectacle, a flypast of bird power. In flight they offer photographers time to focus and capture their majesty. White birds bathed in sunlight are better photographed underexposed to bring out feather detail that would otherwise be lost. The greatest number of feathers recorded on a single swan is

over 25,000, 40 per cent of which were on the head and neck. Winter and spring, with the arrival and departure of migrating birds, are the seasons that emphasise the strength of the bird.

Like a modern aircraft, its elegant exterior covers a light frame. Unlike diving birds swans are constructed to minimize weight, trimmed for take-off. Their bones are pneumatized, containing many air-filled cavities that communicate via an air-sac system.[2] Peoples such as the Lapps have fashioned flutes from such long, hollow limb bones. Nevertheless, it needs a long stretch of water for take-off. It has to run along the surface for 5 metres (17 feet) or more, flapping its wings and beating the water with its feet to gain enough momentum to launch into the air. Its feet give extra vertical force to keep the bird out of the water, providing forward thrust to aid the wings.

Economy is also achieved by formation flying. By flying just outside the wingtip vortices created by its neighbours, a bird in a v-formation can exploit the wake upwash generated by the vortices. In effect it captures some of the energy contained in the rotating air, and uses this to make its own flight easier, perhaps reducing the power needed for cruising flight by as much as 15 per cent.[3] Swans have the power to sustain long-haul flights at speed. Landing is a simple process, deceleration through a

In 1956 five Scandinavian nations with swans as their emblem marked Northern Countries Day by issuing similar stamps.

pattering motion of the feet acting as a reverse thrust. Indeed, in 1936 the French poet Paul Valéry credited a Renaissance genius with a dream of carrying man aloft: 'Leonardo da Vinci . . . inventa l'homme volant . . . monté sur son grand cygne'.[4]

Swans at rest present opportunities for pleasing reflections in the water, as the poet Thomas Hood observed:

> There's double beauty whenever a swan
> Swims on a lake, with her double thereon.[5]

In the same family as ducks and geese, Anatidae, the swan is visually closer to the goose. To confuse them though is to misjudge their comparative value. The belletrist Horace Walpole made the distinction clear in his comment on the artist Sir Joshua Reynolds: 'All his own geese are swans, as the swans of others are geese.'[6] The eighteenth-century statesman and political philosopher Edmund Burke had to endure taunts con-

Swans are image-makers.

cerning his Irish origin. In the press he was Edmund Bonny Clabber 'the goose turned swan by the inspiring streams of the Liffey and the Shannon'.[7] In discussing whether a writer's work has stood the test of time, a distinction is sometimes drawn between a 'literary swan' and a 'village goose'. With a novelist's eye Elizabeth Gaskell commented of Florence Nightingale:

> She must be a creature of another race so high & mighty & angelic, doing things by impulse – or some divine inspiration & not by effort & struggle of will. But she sounds almost too holy to be talked about as a mere wonder. Miss Nightingale [i.e. Florence's long-suffering sister Parthenope] says – with tears in her eyes that they are ducks & have hatched a wild swan.[8]

The term is now well known as the title of Jung Chang's 1991 account of three daughters, *Wild Swans*, covering the tribulations of three generations of political upheaval in twentieth-century China.

Unlike colourful drakes and ducks, swans have at first sight an equality of the sexes. White or black, their plumage is the same, male (cob) or female (pen). Males tend to be bigger than females. Otherwise differences between the sexes, for example the colour or form of the bill, are only evident on a closer view. Their offspring, cygnets, a Norman-French term for swan, are grey-brown when born, gradually growing into a single colour.

Adult courtship ritual involves posturing tenderly head to head, with mutual preening and drinking and feeding displays. Preening, through the release of fluid from an oil gland, reconditions, cleans and waterproofs the feathers. After copulation, other mutual displays involve lifting neck and wings and calling loudly.

How do swans mate in water? Fluid could vitiate successful insemination. To survive as a genus, as part of their evolution, ducks, geese and swans have all developed a penis. This is normally concealed within the cob's body but protrudes during copulation.[9] Black swans in Australia, which do not migrate, mate twice a year, in spring and autumn.

Nests on riverbanks and the shores of lakes and ponds are far from elegant, an untidy heap of grass, sedges and moss about 2 metres across and half a metre high to keep the eggs clear of water. The twentieth-century poet Norman MacCaig referred to 'a swan's throne' as 'a heap of trash'.[10] Birds bite off material such as reeds and simply throw it down, letting it sink under its own weight before the pen scoops out a central depression. Elevation of the nest also provides a lookout against predators. These include birds such as crows, gulls and owls, enemies in the water such as pike and snapping turtles and various land creatures: badgers, bears, coyotes, foxes, mink (which can also swim), raccoon, snakes and squirrels. These eat eggs and cygnets or leave bites that may become infected.

For just over a month, in untidy nests, pens turn their eggs to keep them uniformly warm.

Cobs patrol the nesting area to guard against unwelcome visitors, taking the pen's place on the nest to keep the eggs warm in the lining of down from her breast when she leaves it to feed and preen. Like other birds the pen turns the eggs with her beak to keep them evenly warm. Usually the clutch of pale and unmarked eggs, typically six, hatches within a day and, under watchful parental eyes, the short-necked cygnets leave the nest a day later for the water. As Shakespeare observed,

Parent mute swans (*Cygnus olor*) calmly watch over cygnets, turning aggressive with predators.

> So doth the swan her downy cygnets save,
> Keeping them prisoners underneath her wings.[11]

Sometimes, protecting themselves from attack by large fish below, the young ride on their mother's back until they are brave enough to form a compact flotilla in her wake. Both parents take part in rearing them over six months, pulling up weed for food. Should cygnets be orphaned, as has happened when the pen has been killed by vandals, a mother goose has been known to take over their care, being accepted by the cob.

By six months – times vary by species – they learn to fly. Grey down turns to brown and remains mottled for two years or so before becoming adult one-colour plumage. Flight feathers develop at around five months. At this time, on long-distance migrations, young birds are at their most vulnerable. The surviving young may remain with parents until they are ready to choose a mate.

This process is programmed to avoid too much inbreeding. Research has shown that young swans have certain beak details in common with their parents. Dark patches on the beaks of parents and cygnets are similar in shape. When choosing a mate young swans tend to select partners with markings different from those of their parents. Recognition that was useful in family bonding as a cygnet has become a means of healthy pairing with a partner not closely related.[12] In contrast, some groups of Canada geese have become so inbred on sites such as municipal lakes that they have grown deformed wings.

Almost entirely vegetarian, swans feed by dabbling, not diving, for aquatic plants such as duckweed and eelgrass. Their long necks reach deeper waters than ducks, enabling their strong bills to pull out starchy roots and tubers. Small food items such as insects and snails for protein, necessary when breeding, and fish eggs (to the chagrin of anglers) are also eaten from the bottom of ponds. Grasping and tearing plants is easy with bills that have serrated edges for straining water and a nail at the tip. The surface of the tongue is spinous. Having depleted aquatic vegetation, some species invade arable land to feed on cereals, turnips, oilseed rape and early spring grazing, to the annoyance of farmers. Low voltage electric fencing, occasional bangers and patrolling dogs are an answer.

Swans are relatively long-lived. A typical lifespan in the wild is about 20–30 years, longer, as much as 50 or more, in captivity. Pairs bond from the age of two and mature at three and four. Followers of tradition, generally they will remain in familiar territory. Each spring bonded pairs return to the same nesting sites to breed, coming back in the autumn to their warmer wintering grounds, large lakes and bays. Hence the saying 'It is seldom that the white swan has not white weather in his wake' is, like many weather saws, inaccurate. During the midsummer moult they are flightless, more at risk from predators. Cobs and pens moult at different times so that one can fly while the other stays with the cygnets.

In the seasonal migrations, flights for survival, young swans travel with their parents, learning landmarks along the route and where feeding is possible in groups at staging posts on lakes, rivers and salt marshes. Feeding renews reserves of fat, fuel for the flight, the engine being breast muscles keeping the wings beating steadily. Migration tends to be at night, leaving the day for rest and recuperation. Night air is cooler, denser with a lower likelihood of headwinds. Lower temperatures and higher humidity also reduce loss of water from the body through evaporation. Mental maps are carried over from season to season. Humans log the flights across the latitudes via orbiting satellites tracking signals from miniature radio transmitters clipped to feathers.

Swans live chiefly in regions with a mild or cold climate, native to every continent except Africa and Antarctica. So widespread were they that in English they have a variety of collective nouns: a bank, a bevy (also used of larks and quails) or an eyrar (derived from eyrie) of swans; a drift, a game, a herd, a lamentation (taken from the legend of the dying swan's last lament), a sownder, whiting, or team.[13] Thus John Dryden's heroic couplet:

Like a long team of snowy swans on high
Which clap their wings and cleave the liquid sky.[14]

Wedge, describing the formation, is generally used of birds in flight. In Britain they are wildfowl; in the USA the term waterfowl is used.

The five species in the Northern hemisphere have white plumage; the three in the Southern hemisphere generally have some degree of black. Behaviour of the eight extant species also varies. The most common is the mute swan, native to northern Europe and Asia but introduced to North America, where it flourishes. A quiet, elegant bird, its s-shaped neck has more vertebrae, 23 freely moving saddle-shaped joints, than any other warm-blooded animal.[15] Its appearance and name, however, belie its nature. When angry, it hisses and snorts, perhaps trumpets feebly. In the breeding season the cob increases its body size, and hence its threatening appearance, by arching its wings and ruffling its scapular feathers. Working together, its two feet create a bow wave as it surges forward in the water to mount an aggressive defence of its staked-out territory. Such a display avoids actual fighting and injury; rearing out of the water, it can drive away rivals and other wildfowl.

Vicious fighting between species is not unknown. Mute swans have been so long established at Brayford Pool in the heart of Lincoln that legend has it, if they ever leave, the city's eleventh-century cathedral will fall down. A local Swan Preservation Society looks after them. In 2004, when there were over 150 resident swans, some black competitors appeared from an unknown source, possibly escapees from a private collection. Although the newcomers were smaller in size and about one-tenth the number of their opponents they were regarded as dirty fighters, going for the throat to force an enemy neck under water. Straying cygnets were particularly at risk. Dabchicks and grebes can get away with tweaking the tail feathers of a swan for devilment, diving under water before the much larger bird can retaliate.

Its wings are able to break a human limb, for example the arm of a child teasing it. Serene when undisturbed, swans can become savagely aggressive when they sense their mate and cygnets are at risk. They can get very stressed when near cats and dogs, especially during the breeding season. In May 2004, for example, seeing a springer spaniel swimming and chasing wildfowl in what it regarded as its park pond, a cob rushed

The Threatened Swan is one of the masterpieces by Dutch painter Jan Asselijn (c. 1610–1652). It captures the aggression of a swan defending its nest against an approaching dog.

forwards hissing and loomed over its enemy. With its powerful wings the swan battered the dog into submission and then its beak held the stunned animal underwater until it drowned. Two minutes later the body floated to the surface and drifted to the bank, where the distraught owner, who had been yelling at his pet to get out of the water, retrieved it.[16] If a swan is injured and has to be rescued, it has to be temporarily smothered to prevent it spreading its wings and then manoeuvred into a canvas or similar bag with an opening for its head.

A distinguishing feature of the mute swan is its bright orange flattened bill with a black knob on the upper part near its eyes. The knob is larger on the cob than on the pen. In flight its wings produce a deep throbbing hum, which has been likened to the whine of a humming top. This noise, made by the stiff outer wing feathers, may be useful for keeping in contact and also help in avoiding collisions during night flight. Other species have their recognizable calls. Reputedly the exhilarating rhythm of mute swan wing-beats inspired Wagner when in 1856 he began composing the music for *Die Walküre* (*Ride of the Valkyrie*).[17] In the age of the mobile phone this has become a ringtone. The poet and writer Laurie Lee noted his impression of an air raid in his 1944 diary, describing 'the wicked hum of falling shrapnel which has many sounds from a piercing whistle to a low savage beating of swan's wings'.[18]

Mute swan is a contradiction in terms philologically. In the Indo-European family of languages, going as far back as the Sanskrit *svanos*, the word swan has a root meaning of 'sound', which may refer to its wing beat. The word occurs particularly in the Germanic languages such as Old Norse, Danish and Old Frisian. In Anglo-Saxon, for example, *swinsian* means to make melody. Nevertheless the Elizabethan poet Sir Philip Sidney (1554–1586) regarded the bird as silent:

Dumb swans, no chatt'ring pies [magpies], do lovers prove,
They love indeed, who quake to say they love.[19]

Until 1785, when it was renamed by the naturalist Thomas
Pennant in his *Arctic Zoology*, the mute swan was known as the
tame swan, having become almost domesticated.

Man's attempted dominance over nature was evident in the
formation from the mid-nineteenth century of acclimatization
societies. Their purpose was to introduce animals and plants to
foreign environments where they would flourish as domestic
stocks. The movement was particularly strong in the British
Empire, which covered a quarter of the world's land surface and
offered many opportunities for the exchange of species. For
example, New Zealand had more acclimatization societies than
any other country and Australia came second. Through the work
of the Acclimatisation Society of the United Kingdom, founded
in 1860, and its sister societies in Australia and New Zealand, the
mute swan was exported. At first the Acclimatisation Society of
Victoria was unsuccessful in introducing the species. Later there
was more success on the other side of the continent. Three pairs
of mute swans, the gift of the Worshipful Company of Vintners
in London, were landed at Perth in 1897. Four years later their
offspring 'were turned out for acclimatisation' in Western
Australia. A breeding population survived to compete with the
indigenous black swans. Mute swans were established in New
Zealand in the late 1860s through the activity of the Otago
Acclimatisation Society, founded in 1864.[20]

Noisier than the mute swan are the whooper and Bewick's
swan, both once regarded as wild swans as against the tame.
The whooper swan of Europe and Asia is a shy bird with a loud,
assertive trumpeting call not unlike the sound of a bugle. Other
observers have compared it to the playing of a trombone, even

Whooper swan (*Cygnus cygnus*, centre) with larger mute swan cousins.

to silver bells. Too much must not be made of such comparisons. Swan vocalizations, unlike those of songbirds, are simple. In its shyness the whooper chooses secluded breeding sites that it stoutly defends. In flight it is relatively quiet, its wing beats making a swishing sound in contrast to the 'wing music' of the mute swan. It differs too in having a yellow patch on its bill and holding its long, thin neck straight.

Not until 1830 was Bewick's swan, named after Thomas Bewick (1753–1828), a celebrated English wood-engraver who specialized in animal illustrations, recognized as a species distinct from the whooper. It was zoologist William Yarrell (1784–1856) who recognized the smaller-sized bird and the lighter yellow on its bill. Like the whooper, Bewick's swan is a migrant from the Arctic. The smallest of the northern swans, in shape it is more like a goose. Its neck is shorter than the whooper's and its head more rounded with a smaller yellow patch. The pattern of yellow and black on its bill is peculiar to each bird, making it possible for ornithologists to identify individual birds and follow their behaviour year after year. The Bewick cry is a distinctive high-pitched honk, clear and strong. In mass flight it can be heard over a distance of several kilometres.

The largest swan is the North American trumpeter, so called from the resonant deep call that emanates from its long trachea. The many bends in it are in effect not unlike the curves in a French horn. An adult male has a wingspan of about 3 metres, is about 1.7 metres long and can weigh 12 kilograms or more. It rivals the great bustard in being the heaviest flying bird. Trumpeters and whoopers are believed to have evolved from a

A Bewick's swan (*Cygnus bewickii*, right) with a larger mute swan to left.

A pair of trumpeter swans (*Cygnus buccinator*).

common ancestor, separating probably during one of the Ice Ages, as did Bewick's and the whistling swan. These two species do interbreed. A large black-billed bird, the whistling swan was discovered and named by explorers Meriwether Lewis and William Clark in 1806, at the end of their transcontinental expedition to find a good route to the Pacific. They perhaps took the sound cue from the naturalist Thomas Pennant. Whistling as an attribute may have resulted from either the bird's high-pitched call or from the sound of its wings in flight. Its accuracy as a description of the call is disputed. Calls are various: honking, clanging and a soft musical 'oo-oo-oo' accentuated in the middle.

This trumpeter cygnet is destined to grow into the largest of the swan species.

The species was only recently renamed the tundra swan.

There is no movement of swans between hemispheres. In the Southern hemisphere Australia has the black swan, which has sooty-black feathers with white wing tips and a red bill. White flight feathers are conspicuous only when the bird is flying. Although it is the state emblem of Western Australia it is found throughout the southern parts of the country, running

The North American tundra swan (*Cygnus columbianus*) was originally called the whistling swan.

Black swans
(*Cygnus atratus*),
one of the unusual
species of
Australian wildlife.

Elegant in water,
out of it the swan
looks ungainly.

through folklore. There are Aboriginal stories about tribal people who began life as black swans and were turned into men. Another version has the bird originating in a black duck that got its head stuck in a hollow mangrove. As the duck tried to free itself, its neck stretched and its beak turned blood-red. The black swan was introduced to New Zealand in 1864 by the Auckland Acclimatisation Society, the first wildfowl to be imported. Four years later offspring were reported on lakes and rivers on the Auckland Peninsula. Before 1864 the species was introduced to South Island by the Nelson Acclimatisation Society. Later in the decade the Otago and Southland Societies introduced the bird to the other end of South Island.[21] Being reasonably tame, it has been exported all over the world as an ornamental bird. Black swans tend not to claim an individual territory like other species and prefer to nest in colonies.

Following the *rara avis* comment of the Roman satirist Juvenal,[22] a black swan became a proverbial term for something extremely rare or even non-existent. It was first reported to the western world by the Dutch explorer Willem de Vlamingh in 1697. For many years it was still regarded as a rare bird. Thus John Wesley, the founder of Methodism, noted in his journal on 2 October 1764, 'I breakfasted with Mr B—, a black swan, an honest lawyer!'[23]

South America has two pink-legged forms. The black-necked swan, inhabiting the southern part of the continent, is a beautiful but ill-tempered bird. Its body is white, its head and neck black with a prominent fleshy outgrowth on the bill. The species is comparatively light, a female weighing around 4 kilograms. Its beauty made it an early candidate for acclimatization in other lands such as Australia and Britain. Smallest of the swans is the all-white coscoroba, onomatopoeically named by the native Indians for its call, 'cos-cor-oo-ba'. The species is

The black-necked swan of South America (*Cygnus melancoryphus*) looks like a half-breed between Australia and the Northern hemisphere.

The all-white South American coscoroba (*Coscoroba coscoroba*) is the smallest of the eight surviving swan species.

regarded as an intermediate between whistling ducks and true swans. Its neck is short. Being small and light, the coscoroba can take off without having to run to gain lift-off speed.

In addition to the surviving eight species – ornithologists disagree on seven or nine according to classification – four extinct breeds are known. Most of them have been found on islands. Having heard Maori speak of the Pouwa bird that they had driven from the Te Whanga lagoon on Chatham Island 800 kilometres east of New Zealand, E. O. Forbes discovered a giant swan fossil there. The last specimen is believed to have died in about 1590. Possibly the breed was the ancestor of the black swan. Last observations of the Mascarene swan, so called from the Indian Ocean Islands, were about 1668 on Mauritius and about 1670 on Réunion. Its disappearance was attributed to the introduction of rats, cats, and pigs; deforestation and hunting also contributed to extinction, as later for the sprinting tortoise. The giant swan of Malta dates from the Pleistocene era, 1.8 million years ago. Remains of other swans in association with flamingo fossils have been discovered near Fossil Lake, Oregon. Fossil records of the swan family go back over 80 million years to the late Mesozoic era.

In migration, species have their chosen routes. Tundra swans migrate the farthest. Those that winter along the Pacific seaboard in California valleys fly some 4,500 kilometres (2,800 miles) to the Alaskan breeding grounds. Migration from Alaska and Arctic Canada via Wisconsin, Lake Michigan, Lake Ontario and Pennsylvania to the eastern seaboard of the US, Chesapeake Bay and the marshes of Virginia and North Carolina, means covering some 6,100 km (3,800 miles). Monitoring exact routes and times is important for bird lovers in identifying hazards and conserving staging sites along flight paths. When tundra swans leave their winter homes on the Atlantic seaboard they are at their lowest body weight of the year and it is important that they are able to add fat and protein at stopovers along the migratory route. Survey results are also indicators of changing weather patterns, especially global climate change.

Whooper swans have shorter routes. The Icelandic group overwinters in the UK and Ireland while the Scandinavian and Siberian birds migrate to Western Europe. Flights, ideally with a tailwind, can last up to 14 or 15 hours at cruising speeds of about 65 kilometres (40 miles) per hour and altitudes of 300–600 metres (984–1968 feet). Speeds and altitudes vary, depending upon factors such as headwinds and cloud cover. In bad weather the birds fly close to the ground.

From early September flocks of Bewick's swan, a high Arctic breeder, leave the Russian tundra before it freezes over to winter mainly in the Netherlands and UK. Their staging posts on the 3,000–3,500 kilometre (1864–2175 miles) journey are two or three, in Estonia, the Gulf of Finland and the White Sea area. Appropriately the music *Swan Flight* by the Estonian composer Veljo Tormis (born 1930) has been recorded by the Estonian–Finnish Symphony Orchestra. Arrival of Bewick swans in northwest Europe is usually from mid-October; return migration begins in February. Timing depends upon temperature. Bewicks can tolerate temperatures a few degrees below zero but colder than average weather can force them from snowy Siberian wastes to warmer climes. Migration in significant numbers is an indication that snow cannot be far behind. To the East birds have a separate route, to Japan, China and Korea. In the favoured winter home of south-west Korea farmers used to believe that large numbers of swans flying in was auspicious, portending a rich harvest. Chen Shanwei Swan Lake, Rongcheng, Shandong Province in north-east China is known as the Eastern Kingdom of Swans. Occasionally, in severe winters, very rare stragglers, vagrants blown off course, have arrived in northern India.

A well-known winter habitat in Japan is Magi Lake in Shimoda Park, on a peninsula to the south west of Tokyo. In March, when the swans are about to depart for Siberia, Shimoda town sponsors a Swan Day Festival. It's a family day out. Activities include feeding the birds ready for their journey, a photographic competition and a swan impersonation contest. Children of all ages can look through a hole in a painting and have a fun photograph taken of themselves riding on a swan. Flight performance varies by species. It has been shown, for example, that on short-distance foraging flights (2–10 kilometres or up to 6 miles) trumpeter swans fly at lower altitudes and more slowly than tundra swans. Moreover, the total energy needed for such flights is some 150 per cent more for a trumpeter than a tundra. Hence the trumpeter, even when it is native to an area, is either less inclined to fly or in flight is an easier target for hunters.[24] This is borne out by the near-extinction of the species in the nineteenth and early twentieth centuries. Fortunately, along with other swan species, they have survived. Swans, with their many admirable qualities, widely appreciated, also survive beyond their natural history and across a larger area in the more permanent worlds of art, literature and music.

2 Grace and Favour

Close observation of species dates from the early nineteenth century, building on the work of Carolus Linnaeus, the eighteenth-century Swedish taxonomist who had established the principles of scientific classification of plants and animals. During the Enlightenment and the Romantic period, observers of the natural world such as Gilbert White (1720–93) largely worked in isolation, communicating with friends. The early nineteenth century was a time of more systematic observation, recording and classification in the sciences. Investigations were international. In Britain the wood-engraver Thomas Bewick produced the drawings for *Water Birds* (1804), the second volume of his *History of British Birds*. Regarded as Bewick's finest work, by 1847 it was in its eighth edition.

In 1827, near the end of his life, Bewick was visited by the American naturalist John Audubon (1785–1851), who before the meeting reckoned Bewick's wood-engravings 'superior to anything ever attempted in ornithology'.[1] Audubon, who sought publication of his bird drawings, had been advised to go to Europe, where he would find engravers with higher skills and a more sympathetic reception from patrons and publishers. Robert Havell the younger, a London engraver, published Audubon's illustrations in four volumes as *The Birds of America* (1827–38). The accompanying text, *Ornithological Biography* (1831–9) in five volumes and a single-volume index, was mainly the work of the Scottish naturalist William MacGillivray. A smaller seven-volume edition of Audubon's *Birds of America* was produced in New York (1840–44). The original books with their high quality large colour plates, which were sold by soliciting subscriptions, became collectors' items.

MacGillivray himself produced over the last fifteen years of his life *A History of British Birds*, his classification based on their anatomical structure. Audubon, who was also interested in anatomy and used rum to preserve swan remains for analysis, considered the work the best of its kind in English. Another Scottish ornithologist, Alexander Wilson, established an earlier scientific line of books on American birds, producing seven volumes from 1808 to 1813. After his death in 1813 the eighth and ninth volumes were completed by his assistant George Ord, and the work was continued from 1828 to 1833 by C. L. Bonaparte, a nephew of the Emperor Napoleon. In the twentieth century the outstanding artist, ornithologist and conservationist of wildfowl was Sir Peter Scott. The son of Scott of the Antarctic, Peter gave his first one-man show of paintings at the age of twenty-four. His prime hobby was wildfowling and this was to remain his main artistic subject. Observing geese in their migrations during the late 1930s, he became increasingly interested in conserving rather than shooting them. In 1946 he founded at Slimbridge by the River Severn in Gloucestershire, the Wildfowl Trust, since renamed the Wildfowl and Wetlands Trust (WWT). A Site of Special Scientific Interest, being among other things a winter refuge for Bewick's swans, Slimbridge became a model for developing further sites that would attract visitors.

Altogether there are now nine WWT centres in the UK covering around 2,000 hectares where wildfowl are bred and studied. Like Slimbridge, some have a wildlife art gallery in which chosen artists provide insights into animal behaviour and habi-

J. J. Audubon's *American Swan*, i.e. a trumpeter, was 'drawn from nature' in the early 1840s.

tats. Peter Scott, knighted in 1973, made several expeditions to study wildlife in places such as the Canadian Arctic, Iceland, Australasia and the Pacific. Presenting programmes on television and writing books, among them *The Swans* (1972) with the Wildlife Trust, he did a tremendous amount to popularize natural history. Through such media members of the public were able to learn about the bird's behaviour, adding to their appreciation of what may have seemed merely an elegant creature.

Some birds have a single attribute: hawk eye; thieving magpie; singing blackbird; wise owl; cuckoo in the nest. Others are ambivalent: crows bad or lucky omens; doves symbols of peace or pests eating crops; falcons clever birds of prey but for racing pigeon owners a menace. The swan has many attributes and associations, many of them pre-dating close observation. Some are superficial, flights of fancy, suppositions long held to be true. They have inspired poetry and fable, not always with a happy ending. There are frequent associations with death, the approach of which the bird itself is believed to be well aware as it sings its swansong. Almost every attribute has its contrast, perfection its sinister aspect. The existence of black and white swans, long conjectured, provoked philosophic discussion not only of moral purity but also in hard logic. Because no philosopher had seen a black swan, was it true that 'all swans are white'?

For most people mention of swans immediately conjures up a picture of beauty, dignity, elegance, grace and tranquillity. The birds are wholly admirable. Adjectives are superfluous. The attributes are there in swan-necked, a swan dive, a swan-shaped bed. The mistress, or wife according to Danish law – she bore him six children – of King Harold II, who was defeated at Hastings in 1066, was Edith Swan-neck. Oscar Wilde conjured up a one-sentence picture in his early fairy tale 'The Remarkable Rocket': 'The sledge was shaped like a great golden swan, and between the swan's wings lay the little Princess herself'.

A late-19th-century German silver centrepiece or *jardinière*.

To swan about, in or off, originally military terms from early in the Second World War, have a pejorative sense but most references are associated with beauty. In Henry James's 1878 novel *Confidence* 'graceful, innocent, amusing' Blanche 'had quite the plumage of a swan, and sailed along the stream of life with an extraordinary lightness of motion'.[2] Rosamond Lehmann described new bride Tanya in her 1944 novel *The Ballad and the Source*:

> She wore a dress of stiff white silk flaring around the ankles into wavy rows of pleated flouncing, with an overskirt of white gauzy stuff, swept up to pile all its puffed fullness into the back, and caught here and there among its folds with bunches of blue and white buds. When she moved, it was a swan moving, and the sound she made was of stirred rushes.[3]

The Times obituary of socialite and writer C. Z. Guest (1920–2003), one of the beautiful people, captured her essence: 'Mrs Winston Guest was a survivor of that bright New York world described by Truman Capote as one of "enduring swans gliding upon waters of liquefied lucre".'[4] To Wordsworth it was not quite so elegant. In his autobiographical poem *The Prelude* (1805) he writes:

> . . . lustily
> I dipped my oars into the silent lake,
> And, as I rose upon the stroke, my boat
> Went heaving through the water like a swan.[5]

It is a poetic bird, frequently referred to in poems and the inspiration for many individual poems. When Apollo, god of poetry

These large 19th-century stone sculptures are below the parterre at Waddesdon Manor, Buckinghamshire, which houses the Rothschild Collection.

and prophecy, was born on Delos on the seventh day of the month, seven being the number of perfection, sacred swans flew seven times round the island before Zeus presented him with his lyre. A beautiful young man, he was accompanied by an equally beautiful male swan and the bird came to represent the powers of poetry and the divinely inspired poet himself. Milton included it on the fifth day of creation in *Paradise Lost* (1667):

> . . . the swan, with arched neck
> Between her white wings mantling proudly, rows
> Her state with oary feet.[6]

Poetic inspiration has persisted until modern times, for instance in *Les Cygnes*, an 1887 Symbolist collection by the American-born French poet Francis Viélé-Griffin. In 1929 the Icelandic poet Jóhannes Bjarni Jónasson published *The Swans*

Are Singing, a Neoromantic lyrical love of nature. Multiple narrators of *Le Chronique du Cygne* (1949) by the Belgian poet Paul Willems tell an allegorical tale of paradise found.

The year before he produced his best known painting *The Scream* (1893), the tortured Norwegian artist Edvard Munch painted *Vision,* consisting of a scream-like head beneath a swan and its reflection. The oil painting is a contrast between the perception of an awful darker reality in the present and what might be better at some time in the future, but even that is uncertain, perhaps a false promise. Returning to the subject four years later in a pen and ink study, Munch wrote:

> I lived deep down among slime and creatures – I forced myself up to the water surface, longing for the bright colours – A dazzling white swan was gliding over the shining surface – reflections of its serene contours in the water – which also mirrored the bright clouds in the sky – I stretched out my hands to reach it – begged it to come. But it was unable to, could not penetrate the circle of mud and slime surrounding me – its head and chest became dirty and it glided away.

At the time Munch was unhappy with women and was warding off their threats with alcohol. He was the great Symbolist, an outsider who regarded the artist as victim, a continual prey to emotional crises in which he could nevertheless revel.

After the Russian Revolution the disillusioned poet Marina Tsvetaeva, whose husband was one of the first to fight with the White Russians in the south against the Bolsheviks, wrote in her unheated Moscow garret a series of poems, *The Camp of Swans* (1917–21). In them she portrayed beautiful Sergei, the one person she could not live without, as a hero:

Tapestries like this 19th-century Russian example gave scope for depicting large birds.

White Guards: Gordian knot
Of Russian valour.
White Guards: white mushrooms
Of the Russian folksong.
White Guards: white stars,
Not to be crossed from the sky.
White guards: black nails
In the ribs of the Antichrist.[7]

The Mexican poet González Martínez mounted a concise attack on the excesses of poetic modernism in his 1911 sonnet 'Tuércele el cuello al cisne de engañoso plumaje' ('Wring the neck of the swan with the false plumage'). For him the swan was a deceitful bird, a superficial symbol with a hollow elegance. In its artificial aestheticism it did not feel the soul of things or the voice of the landscape. That did not deter John Hollander, who in 1969 wrote a concrete poem, 'Swan and Shadow', in which the bird and its reflection adorn the page.

The swan has been likened to a white galleon, a haughty ship. James Elroy Flecker (1884–1915) had a similar view: 'I have seen old ships sail like swans asleep.'[8] In 1820 Shelley was more ethereal:

My soul is an enchanted boat,
Which, like a sleeping swan, doth float
Upon the silver waves of thy sweet singing.[9]

In yoga the swan pose, *hamsasana*, is a stretch in which all the weight of the body finally rests on the hands and tips of the toes. It is a posture that with controlled breathing aims at straightening and strengthening the body, toning the muscles and preventing fatty deposits. In fencing the swan pose was an

Blind and deaf from the age of two, Helen Keller (1880–1968) was nevertheless able to enjoy the company of swans (here, *c.* 1913).

eighteenth-century parrying position in which the hand, wrist and forearm resembled a swan neck, the classic position of the seconde.

Strength goes with beauty. The swan's most powerful limbs are its enormous wings, capable of carrying the bird over hundreds of miles at a stretch. In Vedic literature, the Hindu sacred books, it is depicted as a wide-winged bird, a symbol of the soul liberated and soaring upwards to the heights of our being. Thus the bird regarded from its plumage as a living manifestation of light is also a creature of enlightenment, which can be obtained through poetry or meditation in a yoga position.

Allied to strength is longevity, caught by Alfred, Lord Tennyson in his poem on *Tithonus* (1860), granted immortality but not perpetual youth:

The woods decay, the woods decay and fall,
The vapours weep their burthen to the ground,
Man comes and tills the field and lies beneath,
And after many a summer dies the swan.

The elegance of the swan makes it an ideal subject in many media. This sculpture in wood, mid-1990s, is by Ian G. Brennan.

In his 1939 novel whose title is taken from Tennyson, *After Many a Summer*, Aldous Huxley wittily dealt with a rich man's attempt to prolong human life indefinitely. Naturalist John Ray stated in his 1676 translation of *Ornithologica* by his fellow naturalist Francis Willughby (1635–1672) that 'It is a very long-lived fowl, so that it is thought to attain the age of three hundred years.' A tenfold exaggeration.

Supposedly swans mate for life, a custom to which Celia alludes in reference to her relationship with Rosalind in Shakespeare's *As You Like It*:

And wheresoe'er we went, like Juno's swans,
Still we went coupled and inseparable.[10]

In fact swans were sacred not to Juno but Venus. They get depressed when kept away from other swans so recovery from an operation is aided by returning them to their kin. Although they have a reputation for refusing to eat and pining to death at the loss of a mate, this may be nothing more than a coincidence of age or weather-related sickness. Separation is not unknown, especially when a domineering cob takes over. There are instances of same-sex pairings, even unusually to the point of building and guarding a nest that will have no eggs. The belief in faith unto death persists, echoed in the saying about a deserted wife: 'She's like a swan. There'll never be another.'

For a bird that has such a limited range of sounds but in keeping with the derivation of its name from a word meaning sound, the swan is regarded as musical. In an Icelandic folk tale a king's son in a forest cave can be made to wake or fall asleep by giantess hags shrieking: 'Sing, sing, my swans.' The Roman poet Lucretius said that 'the short song of the swan is better than

As an artist of the Romantic era, Caspar David Friedrich (1774–1840) gave *Schwane in Schlif* appropriate treatment.

the honking of cranes'.[11] Slightly later, in one of his pastoral poems, Virgil has shepherd-poet Lycidas saying that he 'cackles like a goose among melodious swans'.[12] In his 1579 poem *The Shephearde's Calendar* Edmund Spenser wrote:

He, were he not with love so ill bedight,
Would mount as high, and sing as soote [sweetly] as
    Swanne.[13]

Singing could be life saving, as La Fontaine (1621–1695) related in his fable of the cook and the swan. Having had a drop too much, the cook mistook the swan for the goose and was about to cut its throat when it burst into ravishing song. In the nick of time the cook realized that making such a sweet singer into soup would have been murder. The moral was plain: sweet speech does no harm.[14] Carl Orff's swan in *Carmina Burana* (1936), an operatic setting of a collection of thirteenth-century poems, was not so fortunate. It sang in the oven. Reproducing its anguish, performances are often in a grating falsetto. In Aesop's fable the man who bought a swan in the belief that it would have a beautiful voice was disappointed when it didn't sing to his guests. Only when it was dying did it sing a dirge. Moral: when people won't do something as a favour they sometimes have to do it against their will.[15]

According to Plato, the dying Socrates argued that men mis-represented swans in singing for sorrow, mourning for their own death. Rather, being Apollo's birds, they had the gift of prophecy, a vision of blessings to come. Instead of singing in grief like the nightingale they were rejoicing as they never had before at the imminence of the next world. Socrates would leave this world with as little sorrow as they.[16] Among dying Christian martyrs there was similar spiritual comfort, a happy anticipation of the

LE CIGNE ET LE CUISINIER. Fable LIV.

future life. The superstition of the swansong occurs down the ages in Aristotle, Aeschylus (Clytemnestra before the body of Cassandra in *Agamemnon*), Euripides, Cicero (echoing Socrates), Horace in various *Odes*, Seneca and Martial. One of Martial's epigrams was quoted by the English jurist Sir Edward Coke in the 1600 Case of the Swans: 'The swan murmurs sweet strains with failing tongue, itself the minstrel of its own death.'[17]

At the turn of the 19th century the most famous swans in porcelain were painted by Charles H. C. Baldwyn (1859–1943). Today collectors pay the highest prices for flying swans against a matt blue background.

Shakespeare refers to 'the death-divining swan' in *The Phoenix and the Turtle*, for example, and in *The Rape of Lucrece*:

And now this pale swan in her watery nest
Begins the sad dirge of her certain ending.[18]

In *Othello*, after being stabbed by her husband Iago, Emilia says just before she dies, 'I will play the swan and die in music.'[19] Similarly, in *The Merchant of Venice* when Bassanio is faced with choosing one of the caskets Portia states:

Then, if he lose, he makes a swan-like end,
Fading in music.[20]

In music itself there is Orlando Gibbons's 1612 madrigal:

The silver swan, who, living had no note,
When death approached unlocked her silent throat.

Tennyson, who had written *The Dying Swan*, after the farewell speech in *The Passing of Arthur* went on:

So said he, and the barge with oar and sail
Moved from the brink, like some full-breasted swan
That, fluting a wild carol ere her death,
Ruffles her cold plume and takes the flood
With swarthy webs.[21]

Coleridge, referring to contemporary poetasters, turned an epigram:

Swans sing before they die; 'twere no bad thing
Did certain persons die before they sing.[22]

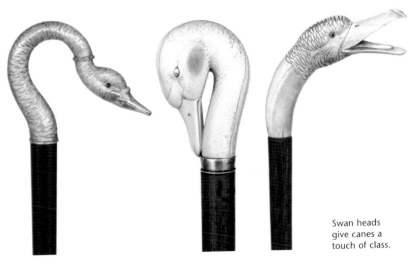

Swan heads
give canes a
touch of class.

The unique Brooke 'Swan Car' was conceived by an eccentric Scottish engineer, R. N. Matthewson of Swan Park, Alipore, Calcutta, and made in England by 1912. It had an eight-note Gabriel horn organ worked off exhaust gases, eyes of coloured prisms that lit up, and a lever-operated opening beak that hissed and sprayed hot water to scatter pedestrians.

Swansong is more than a poetic concept. Ubiquitous, it has been applied to final works and events of all kinds. *Schwanengesang* (1826) was the last book of the Swiss educational reformer Johann Heinrich Pestalozzi (1746–1827), ending in the maxim 'Life itself educates'. Influenced by the ideas of Jean-Jacques Rousseau on developing natural abilities, he died a disappointed man but convinced that his methods would outlive him. Most of them have been accepted in modern elementary education, a posthumous satisfaction.

Swan Song (1946) was a psychological murder mystery by Charles MacArthur (1895–1956) and Ben Hecht (1893–1964); the following year Edmund Crispin wrote a detective story with the same title. *The Song of the Swan* (1998) by Arthur D'Alembert is a science fiction novel in which a message from a supernova in outer space is sent on a 160,000-year journey to earth where, in a science procedural with dates, times and places, human beings struggle to understand the cryptic communication. Is it for the good of mankind or does it mean the end of life on earth?

On his seventieth birthday Mark Twain (1835–1910) said in his speech: 'It's a long time between that first birthday speech and this one. That was my cradle-song, and this is my swan-song, I suppose. I am used to swan-songs; I have sung them several times.'[23] Future celebrities were to retire more than once, on tour, to their benefit. Chekov claimed to have adapted in an hour and five minutes from one of his stories, *Calchas*, a one-act boulevard 'vaudeville', *Swan Song* (1888). The tragic-comic piece takes place on the empty stage of a second-rate provincial the-atre at night after the performance, a benefit night for a sixty-eight-year-old comic actor. He awakes from his alcoholic stupor in his dressing room and, still in the costume of the High Priest of Jupiter in Offenbach's *La Belle Hélène*, looks back on his career. Nikita Ivanich, the prompter, plays up to him that he's still got the talent of when he was the lead in Shakespearean tragedies. The English novelist John Galsworthy chose *Swan Song* for the title of the final book (1928) in the second Forsyte trilogy. Far from being the work of a declining novelist, it has been regarded as among the best of his writing, showing greater social depth, emotional range and narrative subtlety. Although it does not sound so in French, *le chant du cygne d'un artiste*, swansong is now usually a pejorative term, the finale of a back number.

The fateful notion of swans prophesying is not dead. It sur-vives in some German expressions: *mir schwant etwas*, 'I have an uneasy feeling'; *mir schwant nichts Gutes*, 'I have dark forebod-ings, misgivings'. In English, swan as a verb had a milder sense of 'I declare' as a positive exclamation. Thus 'I swan to man' was a way of saying 'I swear to God'. In the nineteenth-century United States swan was slang with a similar meaning. ' I swan if it warn't enough to make a feller dry to see the hogsheads of rum and molasses', wrote Jonathan Slick in *High Life in New York* (1844).

A black-and-white wood engraving by Scottish artist Agnes Miller Parker (1895–1980) multiplies the curves of the swan.

If they have not been swimming in murky water, at least in the northern hemisphere, swans are white. Edmund Spenser laboured the point in the third stanza of *Prothalamion* (1596):

With that, I saw two Swans of goodly hue
Come softly swimming down along the Lee;
Two fairer Birds I yet did never see:
The Snow which doth the top of Pindus strew,
Did never whiter show,
Nor Jove himself when he a Swan would be
For love of Leda, whiter did appear.

The attribute is so demonstrable that it has been used by philosophers in treatises on logic. Aristotle made extensive use of it in *Prior Analytics*, two books on the laws of syllogism. In this form of argument two propositions called premisses contain a common or middle term and the third proposition is the conclusion. This can be false, a piece of crooked thinking. In the first book, for example, Aristotle makes the point:

> It sometimes turns out that B does not necessarily belong to C. Let A be white, B man, C swan. White then necessarily belongs to the swan, but may belong to no man; a man necessarily belongs to no swan.

In *Sophistical Refutations* Aristotle drew attention to fallacies and false syllogisms of the Sophists, known for their ability to conduct specious arguments. A later philosopher, Plotinus (205–270), also used the whiteness of the swan as a readily understandable teaching example in his *Enneads.*

The white swan has its antithesis in the black swan. This was long thought, except in fairy tales, to be a non-existent or rare bird. On account of his dark hair and skin, Ben Jonson described his friend the poet Hugh Holland (1563–1633) as the 'black swan'. Edward Maltby (1770–1859), recently appointed Bishop of Chichester by Earl Grey, who needed his support for the Reform Bill, and the sole Whig in the episcopate, was branded as a 'black swan' when he voted for the Bill in the House of Lords on 8 October 1831.

Storks occur in black and white species but swans have the metaphorical appeal. The duality has become a convenient distinction for philosophers to discuss the process of arriving at the truth. The eighteenth-century empiricist David Hume argued that there were logical problems with induction, generalization from particular observations. Inductive evidence is limited. In *A System of Logic* (1843) John Stuart Mill made the point:

> The course of nature, in truth, is not only uniform, it is also infinitely various . . . To an inhabitant of Central Africa, fifty years ago, no fact probably appeared to rest

on more uniform experience than this, that all human beings are black. To Europeans, not many years ago, the proposition all swans are white, appeared an equally unequivocal instance of uniformity in the course of nature. Further experience has proved to both that they were mistaken; but they had to wait fifty centuries for this experience. During that long time, mankind believed in an uniformity of the course of nature where no such uniformity existed.[24]

Mill went back to Sir Francis Bacon (1561–1626), the founder of inductive philosophy, who condemned the ancients for ascribing a general truth to all propositions that are true in every instance that we happen to know of. Thus for thousands of years, until the European discovery of Australia, 'all swans are white' was believed to be universally true. Proving a proposition false was an example of intellectual progress towards truth. Karl Popper, in *The Logic of Scientific Discovery* (1934), argued for the principle of falsification as a solution to the problem of induction not being able to offer certainty. Much better to adopt a sceptical approach of regarding 'truth' as provisional, the best conclusion on the evidence available so far. Rather than continually trying to prove his theory correct by adding supporting evidence, a process of verification, the scientist should try to disprove it. He should adopt the sceptical approach that a chain is only strong as its weakest link. In logic a scientific statement is conclusively falsifiable although it is not conclusively verifiable.

Does falsification have a practical application? Popper thought that Marxism and psychoanalysis were both pseudo-sciences, intellectual superstitions. There is also a financial angle. An American academic and options trader, Nassim Taleb, argues in 'The Black Swan: Why Don't We Learn What We Don't

Learn', a paper later expanded into the book *The Black Swan* (2005), that events are more random than we perceive. To him black swans are extreme events we are ill equipped for dealing with because of the way our minds work. Black swans occur more often than we bargain for. Not following rules, they are unpredictable, their behaviour almost impossible to forecast. We therefore underestimate the possibility of black swans we know nothing about. In what amounts to a planning fallacy people tend to attribute their failure to ill luck and their success to skills rather than chance. Looking to history for guidance is only a limited view, like a driver keeping an eye on his rear-view mirror while he crashes into the wall in front. There is also the hindsight bias, smart alecs claiming that 'I knew it all along'. Being wise after the event is not difficult; it is accurate foresight that makes for genuine success. Taleb's financial strategy is to bet on rare events, 'black swans', by buying options where he perceives an anomaly in the market that can be exploited. Most of the time he loses his premium because markets tend to move with a herd instinct. When he wins he wins handsomely enough to wipe out his previous losses. He succeeds because the market has failed to price correctly the extreme event; it has failed to recognize the possibility of a black swan.

The immediate association with white is purity. In Norse mythology under the world tree Yggdrasil is the sacred Spring of Urd, which causes everything that comes into contact with it to become 'as white as the film that lies within the eggshell'. On this water live two swans and from them has sprung the whole race of swans; they have their origin in the heart of purity. In folklore young maids are sometimes referred to as swans. In one of Hans Christian Andersen's stories drawn from Scandinavian folklore, 'The Travelling Companion', the image is dark. A bewitched and bloodthirsty maiden appears in the shape of a

Swans in a Royal Doulton figurine, *Endless Love,* are separated by a heart-shaped space.

black swan. It is only when she has been dipped thrice in cleansing water that, released from her spell, she turns into a pure white princess capable of loving her young husband. Because of the assumed purity a fall from grace can be severe. In the traditional folk song *Molly Bond*, probably Irish in origin, a man who has murdered his girl lover tells the court that 'he shot her as a swan'.

The bird has not always been regarded as noble, as exemplified in a mediaeval bestiary compiled *c.* 1220–50, but drawing on earlier treatises and having a definite moral:

> The Latin name of the swan is 'olor', the Greek 'cignus'. It is called olor because it has completely white feathers, and no one has seen a black swan; 'olon' is Greek for 'complete'. It is called cignus for its singing, because it produces sweet songs with a well-tuned voice. It is said that swans can sing so sweetly because they have a long curved neck, and to produce a good singing tone the voice must travel down a long curving path to give a variety of notes. It is said that in the far north, when the

bards sing to stringed instruments, numbers of swans gather and sing together in harmony. Sailors regard them as a good sign; as Ovid's friend Aemilius Macer wrote: 'When you are telling omens by the appearance of birds, to see a swan always means joy; sailors love it because it never dives beneath the waves'. In moral terms, the white plumaged swan represents successful deception; just as the white feathers hide black flesh, so dissimulation hides a sinful heart. When the swan swims on a river it holds its neck high, like a proud man drawn along by the vanity of the world, who glories for a brief time in his possessions. The story of the swans gathering around the bards reminds us that those who live for their desires seek out the company of like-minded men to satisfy their lusts. But when at length the swan dies, it sings very sweetly.

In the same way, when the proud man has to leave this life, he still delights in the sweetness of secular things, and remembers all the evil he has done as he dies. When the swan is plucked of its white feathers, its black flesh can be seen, and it is roasted. In the same way, when the proud rich man dies, he is stripped of worldly pomp and goes down into the flames of hell, where he is plagued with every torment: he who living used to enjoy food is in turn made the food of the flames.[25]

Such mediaeval qualms did not spoil the enjoyment of a group of women in the early twentieth century whose love had its origin in a toy swan. Playing with one in her bath as a small girl, Natalie Clifford Barney (1876–1972), the daughter of an Ohio whiskey heiress and a railway magnate, first became aware of her own sexuality: 'The water that I made shoot between my legs

This swan wallpaper design c. 1875 by the illustrator Walter Crane (1845–1915), shows the influence of Pre-Raphaelite simplicity.

from the beak of a swan gave me the most intense sensation.'[26] Although later she accepted an aristocratic marriage proposal to please her father, lesbian liaisons were natural to her. As she wrote in 1899, 'My queerness is not a vice, is not deliberate, and harms no one.'[27] Her engagement in 1901 was a mere formality and the following year after dreaming of a room filled with flowers for her wedding her father conveniently died, freeing Natalie to live as an American in Paris – in the Belle Époque a paradise for Sapphists.

Dreaming of swans is supposed to reveal the power of the collective mind or the unconscious, the side of human nature usually hidden, the spiritual and the ideal in sexuality. A cruder interpretation is that the white represents virginity in company with the long phallic neck. Interpreters of dreams also argue that swans foreshadow a bereavement or the end of a romance. In truth nobody knows, but it makes entertaining reading in popular magazines.

Close to the concept of purity are the virtues of innocence and chastity. In Hindu beliefs the goddess Sarasvati, who has a swan vehicle, is a spiritual element, the deity of learning and the arts. A *sannyasi* is a religious ascetic who has achieved the fourth *ashrama*, or stage, of life, having renounced the world. The summit of achievement in full self-knowledge is reached over at least twelve years by the *paramahamsa*, the great swan, like the nineteenth-century saint Ramakrishna. In Gaelic Scotland the symbol of the Virgin Mary was the white swan. A Celtic poem with Arthurian characters features a swan brought to court by a sorcerer as a test of chastity, for it will only accept food from the hands of virtuous wives. Naturally it caused some consternation among the women.

In 'Fish in the unruffled lakes' W. H. Auden remarks:

Fish in the unruffled lakes
The swarming colours wear,
Swans in the winter air
A white perfection have.

Praising 'the beauteous Lady Would-be' to the magnifico Volpone in Ben Jonson's play *Volpone* (1606), his parasite Mosca describes her as

A wench
O'the first year! A beauty ripe as harvest!
Whose skin is whiter than a swan, all over![28]

When Jonson was writing, a white complexion was fashionable. In the summer of 1997 dancers booked to appear in the English National Ballet's performances of *Swan Lake* were forbidden to acquire a suntan: 'We simply can't give roasted swans to the public this season.'

Physical attributes of the bird are well caught in Patricia Elliott's novel for children *Ambergate* (2005). Leah, half girl and half swan, has 'the smooth slide of feathers . . . the stiff yet springing shafts, a bony network dividing the softness', which is also heavy 'as if it held the weight of water, like a memory'. In *Heidi* (1881), Johanna Spyri's story of a homeless forlorn Swiss girl trying to make a place for herself in the world, a white goat is Little Swan.

The only play with a conventional romantic love story that August Strindberg wrote was *Swanwhite* (1901). To the tortured pessimist playwright, it was 'an idealistic play of pure beauty, the apotheosis of love'. The heroine Svanevit (Swanwhite) was taken from a Swedish fairy tale in which the stepmother becomes angry when the prince falls in love with the virgin Svanvita instead of her own daughter and so she has him locked up in a tower. In the happy ending to the drama the prince swimming back to Swanwhite drowns, but love is stronger than death. He awakes from the dead through the power of love and is reunited with her. Although it was a bright play based on folk ballads and fairy tales and suitable for a young company, Strindberg had to wait seven years for its première in Finland, when it was accompanied by special music composed by Sibelius.

More successful, certainly commercially, was *The Swan* (1920) by the Hungarian playwright Ferenc Molnár. Its plot is simple: in the lavish 1910 Austro-Hungarian Empire a beautiful princess groomed for the part is betrothed to the crown prince, but she loves her handsome tutor. A romantic comedy, it was an international success in the post-war worlds, being filmed more than once. The glossy 1956 version featured the Hollywood actress Grace Kelly, soon to become Her Serene Highness Princess of Monaco. In the 1990s *The Swan Princess* was twice animated, in 1994 as a reworking of *Swan Lake* and in 1956 as a fantasy about the secret of the castle.

To the Symbolist poet Baudelaire, in the 1861 edition of *Les Fleurs du Mal* (*Flowers of Evil*), the swan represents purity, lost innocence. In a Paris changed out of all recognition by rebuilding after the 1848 revolution, the poet sees a swan that has escaped from its cage on the site of an old menagerie. Bewildered by the absence of water, it seems to reproach God for the lack of rain. In the second part of the poem the swan with its mad gestures brings to the poet's mind a series of images adding up to the misfortunes of mankind, loneliness, loss, defeat, captivity. Beauty and the ills that man is subject to are inseparable.

The black swan in particular has a sinister connotation. In *Anthem for St Cecilia's Day*, dedicated to Benjamin Britten and set to music by him as *Hymn to St Cecilia* (1942), W. H. Auden saw an association with death:

In a garden shady this holy lady
With reverent cadence and subtle psalm,
Like a black swan as death came on
Poured forth her song in perfect calm.

Swan on a Black Sea was a phrase that occurred in the Cummins-Willett scripts, a study in automatic writing, published in a

book of that name (1965).[29] A collection of writings, it was
believed to be by people who communicated with the writer
Geraldine Cummins after their deaths. Willett was the pseudo-
nym of Mrs Charles Coombe Tennant (1874–1956), who herself
had the gift of automatic writing and speech. To one reader, the
book raised the question 'Is there an entity, sometimes called
the soul, that rises like a swan from the black sea of death?'

Still grieving at the untimely death of her daughter Sally,
twenty-four, struck down by polio in 1958 in 'that beastly
Djakarta', the novelist Rosamond Lehmann wrote *The Swan in
the Evening* (1967). In real life she regarded swans as

Bold, greedy, unreliable . . . I can only appreciate them when they rock in midstream like abstract forms of peace and meditation, their cruel heads laid back against sculptured pinions. Even so their blandness is deceptive. At any moment one or another of them will unfold; will ruffle and swell and gather itself and become a charging missile, a death ship propelled by fury up and down the flood. Strange that sexual urges so daemonic should end in such tranquil scenes of domesticity. When they go by in the late summer, each parent couple convoying its mushroom-coloured cygnet fleet, they look as complacent and respectable as a *bourgeois* family on a Sunday outing.[30]

Nevertheless, subtitled *Fragments of an Inner Life*, her testimony along with 'the greatest of the world's great minds' was that 'we are souls travelling in eternity', her 'personal discovery that death does not extinguish life'. If so, that would be the greatest transformation associated with the bird. Its ability to change shape and move from one world to another is legendary.

3 Transformations

The best-known swan transformation is 'The Ugly Duckling', a fairy tale by the Danish author Hans Christian Andersen (1805–1875). Hatched in a duck's nest, the bird is scorned and subjected to various harsh treatments for a whole year until the following spring, when he realizes he is a beautiful bird like the swans he has unknowingly admired. Andersen was fascinated by the imaginative possibilities in swans. He wrote tales about 'The Wild Swans' and 'The Swan's Nest', and many of his other tales contain references to swans, but 'The Ugly Duckling', first published in 1843 in his second collection of fairy tales, became his best-loved story about them.

Andersen was writing not just for children but also for adults, who could appreciate the myths and symbols, the underlying psychology, for the story was in his words 'a reflection of my own life'. In the nature versus nurture debate, nature was the more important to Andersen, the inborn qualities ultimately having more influence than upbringing. As the bird in the story says, 'I never dreamed of so much happiness when I was the Ugly Duckling'. Andersen's early home life in dire poverty had been unhappy; he had been a failure at singing, dancing and acting at the Royal Theatre in Copenhagen; a tall, gangling man with large feet, a hooked nose, awkward movements and a tearful temperament, he was unattractive, particularly to women, who refused his friendship. An outsider who became a compulsive social

The 'Ugly Duckling' has become a universal term variously visualized. These two representations are from a 1913 London edition of Andersen's *Fairy Tales*.

climber, he constantly strove for acceptance, eventually achieving the recognition and admiration he had craved all his life. In 1952 his life story was popularized in film with Danny Kaye in the title role singing songs by Frank Loesser, a continuing hit with children.

Andersen's fairy tales have been translated into 150 languages. One of them is Esperanto, the most successful of the artificial international languages. Its founder, a Polish physician and oculist Dr L. L. Zamenhof (1859–1917), translated the tales himself as well as the *Old Testament*, and classics such as *Hamlet*, the plays of Molière and Goethe. 'The Ugly Duckling' became 'La Malabela Anasido' and 'Swan's Nest' was rendered as 'Cigna Nestro', *cign* derived from Romance languages being the root word in Esperanto. The first edition, 1926, was posthumous.

The outstanding example of a person 'becoming' a swan is the Russian prima ballerina Anna Pavlova (1881–1931). Taken at the age of eight to the Mariinsky Theatre in St Petersburg, home of the Kirov Ballet, for a Christmas performance of *The Sleeping Beauty*, she was immediately enchanted, and set upon becoming a dancer. She also loved animals and birds, as a young woman particularly her pet swan Jack. The grace of Anna and Jack inspired her dancing partner and choreographer Michel Fokine to create in 1905 *The Dying Swan*, which became her symbol. Throughout the piece she was *en pointe*, until the very end, collapsing when the swan dies. Her arms like wings, weakening then still, were more than an impersonation. Anna's strong, skilful performance dramatically stressed the fragility of brief lives, human and animal. On the night of her death her last whispered request was 'Bring me my swan costume . . . play that last measure softly.' The next day her company danced. At the end of their performance the *Swan* music was played as a spotlight roamed over an empty stage. A compilation, *The Immortal Swan*, survives her. It includes shots of her by the ornamental lake with swans at her London home, Ivy House, Hampstead, and extracts from her solo performances filmed by the actor Douglas Fairbanks Sr in Hollywood in 1924.

At the beginning of the twenty-first century an American TV series, *The Swan*, took eighteen plain Janes, and over three months, during which they were deprived of a mirror, a dream team of cosmetic surgeons, dentists, dermatologists, fitness trainers and laser eye specialists gave them a makeover. The winner moved on to The Swan Pageant. To some viewers it was exploitative, showing the self-described ugly ducklings, carefully chosen from several candidates, in the worst 'before' light and promoting unrealistic expectations of 'after'. The whole transformation was costly, beyond most people's resources, and could accentuate psychological difficulties. Critics tended to pan it: 'Queen for a Day with a scalpel' and 'Demeaning to women and birds'. To the mass of viewers though it was a dream made real when reality TV was topping audience ratings. Novelist Maeve Binchy in 1995 was more realistic about such prospects: 'I don't have ugly ducklings turning into swans in my stories. I have ugly ducklings turning into confident ducks.'[1]

Andersen's story 'The Swan's Nest' begins: 'Between the Baltic and the North Sea there lies an old swan's nest, and it is called Denmark. In it have been born, and will be born hereafter, swans whose names shall never die.' He goes on to relate how as flocks of swans the Danes flew from the nest over the Alps to Italy, Byzantium, France, England, Pomerania. An outstanding individual swan was Tycho Brahe (1546–1601), whose detailed observations were the basis of the laws of planetary motion proposed by his assistant Johannes Kepler, who succeeded him as imperial astronomer. In Andersen's own time there were achievers in music, sculpture and literature. It would be a long time before men could say 'That was the last swan! The last swan from the swan's nest!' For the time being Andersen remains the most famous Dane, and the mute swan is the national bird of Denmark.

Before Hans Christian Andersen wrote his stories the German brothers Jacob and Wilhelm Grimm had published three collections of folklore in 1812, 1815 and 1822. One of the tales, 'The Six Swans', is based upon a witch's daughter, an evil queen, turning the king's six sons into swans. They could only be disenchanted by their beautiful sister staying silent for six years and sewing six shirts out of starwort. Married to a king, she maintained her silence and was nearly burnt at the stake through the machinations of her new stepmother but in the nick of time she was saved and the wicked stepmother burnt to ashes instead.

Hans Christian Andersen's 'Wild Swans' features eleven brothers. In a mediaeval French version of this story the king's mother, resenting her fairy daughter-in-law, takes away the necklaces the children were born with, turning them into swans. When the necklaces were restored the children resumed human form, except for the one whose necklace was lost. Remaining a swan, he drew the skiff of his brother, who became the knight of the swan. Thomas Hood's fairy-tale poem 'The Two Swans', tells how one of them was imprisoned in a tower by a serpent until in the form of a tuneful swan 'white Love drew near' and sang, enchanting the serpent. Escaping its pursuit, the two sail to shore

> And change, anon, a gentle girl and boy,
> Locked in embrace of sweet unutterable joy!

The origin of such stories has been traced to the Orient. Fairy stories, as Freud pointed out, are universal, related to day-dreams and wish-fulfilment fantasies. In the rites of passage the questing self encounters high-minded helpers and evil enemies but, after all the trials and tribulations, there is a happy ending. Children reading the 1928 story *Simon the Swan* by the artist and illustrator Cicely Mary Barker or *Swan in the Swim* by Lucy Daniels, in which Mandy is called to get the injured bird back to the Animal Ark before it is too late, may have their apprehensions but behind them is an assurance that everything will turn out all right.

In a secular, scientific age we have not lost our appetite for fantasy. If anything, with the decline of religious belief, it has increased. In the twentieth century two fantasy writers produced their own extensions of Grimm's 'Six Swans'. Nicholas Stuart Gray based his 1962 novel *The Seventh Swan* on the notion that because the sister had run out of cloth the last shirt lacked a sleeve. Thus when the transformation occurred one brother was left with one arm and one wing. In *Swan's Wing* (1981) by Ursula Synge, Countess Almira, the icy beauty who could command snow to fall, was entranced by marvels and freaks of nature. So when she saw the handsome young lord Lothar with the swan's wing instead of an arm she desired him. Under her cold gaze his heart was numbed to the exclusion of everything except the white beauty of the Countess, who called him to her bower at the midnight hour. Her arms opening like a flower welcomed him and he covered her with his wing.

Transformation is a long and widely held tradition associated with swans. The idea occurs in Graeco-Roman, Celtic, Norse, Teutonic and Native American cultures, with versions of basic stories turning up on most continents, even Pacific islands.

The swan appears in many classical legends. Aphrodite (in Roman mythology Venus), the goddess of love, rides in a swan-drawn chariot. As Cycnus (Greek) and Cygnus (Latin) he has

On this Athenian vase of the mid-sixth century BC depicting the Sixth Labour of Heracles (the removal of the Stymphalian man-eating birds), the creatures look uncannily like swans.

various origins and fates. The son of Ares (Mars) and Pyrene, he was turned into a swan when he died. As the son of Poseidon (Neptune), he was born in secret and exposed on the seashore, where he was found by some fishermen who saw a swan flying down to comfort him. He was killed by Achilles before Troy with a well-aimed blow to the head, his only vulnerable part. According to Ovid in his poetic *Metamorphoses*, Cycnus was invulnerable and Achilles choked him to death, whereupon Poseidon changed him into a swan. A king of the Ligurians, son of Sthenelus and a kinsman of Phaeton, whose death he mourned, he became a swan. Ovid describes the process:

> And as he went his voice became thin and shrill; white plumage hid his hair and his neck stretched far out from his breast. A web-like membrane joined his reddened fingers, wings clothed his sides, and a blunt beak his mouth. So Cyncus became a strange new bird – the swan. But he did not trust himself to the upper air and Jove, since he remembered the fiery bolt which the god had unjustly hurled. His favourite haunts were the still pools and spreading lakes; and, hating fire, he chose the water for his home, as the opposite of flame.[2]

Cycnus was also a handsome boy, the son of Apollo by Hyria. Distressed at the desertion of a lover, he drowned himself in what came to be called the Cycnean lake, ever after frequented by swans, into which he and his mother, who also drowned herself, were turned. Apollo, the god of music, related to the bird at birth and death. His birth was attended by a swan, which shared with him the gift of prophecy; his soul was reputed to have passed into a swan, which led to the Pythagorean fable that the souls of all good poets passed into swans.

Hence 'the Swan of Avon', a description of Shakespeare by Ben Jonson. In the late nineteenth and twentieth centuries to 'sling the Swan of Avon' was a slang term for an actor to perform in a Shakespearean play. Major classical poets earned the title: the Swan of Meander was Homer, who is supposed to have lived on the banks of the river; the Swan of Thebes, the lyric poet Pindar; the Swan of Mantua, Virgil, who was born there. In modern times the sobriquet was popular from the seventeenth to the nineteenth centuries: the Swan of Cambrai was the prolific religious writer François Fenelon (1651–1715); the nine-teenth-century Irish soprano Catherine Hayes was the Swan of Erin; the Swan of Lichfield, Anna Seward (1747–1809), who wrote romantic poetry; Voltaire called Francesco Algarotti, eighteenth-century author of popular works on science, art and the classics, the Swan of Padua; the Swan of Usk, Henry Vaughan, a seventeenth-century Welsh religious poet, was born at Newton-by-Usk and an early collection of his poems was entitled *Olor Iscanus* (1651). João da Cruz e Sousa (1861–1898), called Cisne Negro (Black Swan) by his contemporaries, was the leading figure of the Symbolist movement in Brazil. Oksana Baiul (born 1977), the Ukrainian figure skater, took to the ice to the music of *Swan Lake* at the 1994 winter Olympic Games and, in spite of injury the day before, landed five triple jumps. She won the gold medal and was dubbed the Swan of Odessa.

According to Plato, the singer and musician Orpheus, who was torn apart by women, chose in afterlife to be a swan, a musical creature, because he could not consent to be born of woman. The legend that inspired artists and poets is Leda and the swan. Zeus in the form of a swan made love to Leda, who gave birth to an egg from which hatched Helen of Troy ('Was this the face that launched a thousand ships/And burnt the topless towers of Ilium?') and a twin. In one version the twin is Polydeuces, in another Clytemnestra, the faithless wife of Agamemnon. In another version Helen is the daughter of Zeus and Nemesis, god-dess of retribution, who deposited the egg with Leda to bring up as her own child. The egg featuring in both stories suggests that there may have been some earlier tales of gods in the form of birds.

A popular decorative motif, especially in Roman mosaics and sarcophagi, was the visitation of a swan. This classical motif was revived with erotic overtones in the Renaissance depictions of Leda. For instance, the subject inspired a painting by

Anna Pavlova interpreting the death of the swan in *Swan Lake*.

Michelangelo (1475–1564), now lost, but copied in an engraving by Cornelis de Bos *c.* 1563. Michelangelo's pupil Bartolomeo Ammanati (1511–1592) made a marble sculpture, now in the Bargello, Florence, and a painting, *c.* 1530, in the National Gallery, London. In 1865 Sir John Millais bought in Florence what he

Leonardo da Vinci's *Leda and the Swan* is lost, surviving only in copies. This 19th-century lithograph is by Leroux.

thought was a Michelangelo sculpture but was in fact an Ammanati. It is now in the Victoria and Albert Museum.

Also lost is Leonardo da Vinci's 1510–15 painting but there are copies, one for example in the Galleria Borghese in Rome, and his own sketches. Possibly the original, of a full-frontal standing Leda, may have been destroyed because it was considered too erotic. Leonardo's pupil the Florentine painter Jacopo da Pontormo returned to the subject *c.* 1525. Correggio has an elaborate composition of *c.* 1530, now to be seen in the Gemäldegalerie, Berlin, in which Leda is bathing with other women and a swan singles her out. Hans Beham (1500–1550) in Germany and Giulio Bonasone (1498–1558) in Italy both made engravings; Benvenuto Cellini (1500–1571) a gold medallion, now on display in Vienna, and Tintoretto a voluptuous oil now in the Uffizi Gallery, Florence.

Leda and the swan resurfaced as a subject with Rubens in the seventeenth century, whose rich sensual female figure is

Correggio (*c.* 1494–1534) painted this version of Leda and the swan in his later years.

73

entwined with the bird, and Nicolas Poussin in restrained classical style. The Fitzwilliam Museum, Cambridge, has a Soldani Benzi (1656–1740) bronze of about 1717, and in 1742 the French painter François Boucher produced his Rococo version, in which the swan is almost a domestic pet of two flirtatious women. The canvas by Théodore Géricault from the early 1800s, but influenced by Michelangelo and other Renaissance painters, can be seen in the Louvre. In the twentieth century notable artists to revive the subject included the Hungarian Constructivist László Moholy-Nagy, who created a fantasy world in photomontage; Henri Matisse, whose monumental nude Leda beneath the arabesque blue swan is of few colours and lines; and Salvador Dalí. In Dalí's painting begun in 1945, *Leda Atòmica*, the proportions are mathematical. The model, his wife and muse, is set

This 19th-century colour print of Leda and the swan is by an unknown artist.

This German glass bowl showing Leda and the swan dates from the 1920s.

Gouache (body-colour) suited the delicate treatment of mythological subjects by Gustave Moreau (1826–98). Leda was a subject in 1880.

This 1911 etching of Leda and the Swan is by Hans Meid (1883–1977).

with a swan in a pentagon inside which is a five-pointed star, the result being more spiritual than carnal.

Notable modern poets who have written on the theme include Rainer Maria Rilke, D. H. Lawrence, Hilda Doolittle, Robert Graves and W. B. Yeats. The sensual 'Leda and the Swan', much anthologized, by Yeats, begins:

A sudden blow: the great wings beating still
Above the staggering girl, her thighs caressed

By the dark webs, her nape caught in his bill,
He holds her helpless breast upon his breast.

Both Graves and Yeats influenced the Australian artist Sir Sidney Nolan (1917–1992), who painted a Leda and swan sequence. In response to Yeats, American Pulitzer Prize-winning poet Mona Van Duyn (1921–2004) wrote *Leda Reconsidered*. After describing a man receiving radiation treatment for cancer in the song 'Power and Glory' from his 1992 album *Magic and Loss*, Lou Reed is reminded 'of Leda and The Swan and gold being made from lead'. A prose reference based on a painting by Anne Shingleton (b. 1953) occurs in Thomas Harris's 1999 novel *Hannibal*,[3] which dwells on the relationship between the psycho-

Georgiew Wichar's 20th-century painting of Leda and the swan conveys lordly menace.

pathic killer Dr Hannibal Lecter, who leaves one painting in the room uncovered, and the FBI agent Clarice Starling. The artist offers her interpretation of the passage:

> Clarice–Leda has taken vestal vows, has dedicated her body and soul to the FBI . . . Like the life of chaste and virginal Beauty, Clarice's life . . . is manless, and hence . . . arid. The fable now demands that she be sexually fulfilled, 'sexually' having here a wide, deep, polyhedral meaning far beyond mere genital tiddlywinks. Lecter–Swan is a beast. The fable now demands that she make him human, meaning here humane . . . In the book, though alas not in the film, both undergo the magical transformation: Beauty turns the Beast humane, the Beast wafts Beauty to, up and over the moany summit where she is, presumably, fulfilled. Both are reborn from scratch . . . through each other.[4]

Swan maidens have a dual identity. They can become beautiful maidens or swans at will by the simple means of the swan shift, a magical robe of swan's feathers. Common in Germanic and Scandinavian folklore is a tale starting with a hunter espying a group of bathing maidens, typically three or seven. Struck by the beauty of the youngest, he steals her robe, making her unable to fly. Even though she might have married him, she eventually discovers her hidden robe, dons it and escapes. The hunter then either redeems her or, more rarely, dies in desolation.

Variants occur elsewhere. A Romanian version features a king and a singing flute subject to the machinations of an evil gypsy, who thought she had killed the swan maiden. At the crucial moment the flute turns itself into a swan maiden. In a Japanese tale a fisherman argues with a swan maiden about returning her feathery robe after or before she has danced for him. When she claims she cannot dance without it he relents and watches her borne aloft singing sensuous melodies as she enters a cloud drifting towards the summit of Mount Fuji. According to the Buryat folk of Siberia, Khori Tumed surprised maidens – three or nine – bathing in a lonely lake. He took away one's robe, she married him and bore eleven sons. When she asked to try on her old robe he thought he could stop her disappearing through the door of their yurt but she flew up through the smoke hole in the roof, restrained only long enough to name her sons, who became men. Before disappearing for ever to her natural home, the sky, she flew round and round the yurt several times, bestowing blessings and commanding Khori Tumed to celebrate the swans' spring and autumn migrations with special rites.

Theft of female clothing to gain control over her is the basis of other folk tales, which are consistent in their elements. The target in Scandinavian literature is the mermaid and in India the perpetrator is the monkey boy. There is a parallel between swan maidens and the Apsaras of Indian mythology. In the form of swans they swim over the lotus pond of heaven; putting aside their feather dresses they bathe as beautiful females. The houris of the Vedic heaven, they receive into their arms the souls of heroes. Descending to earth, they marry mortals, but their stay is temporary and they have to fly away.

In Celtic myth Oenghus (Angus), the god of love, himself falls in love with a swan maiden, Caer. Every two years on the same day, 1 November, the pagan feast of Samhain, she changed spontaneously into a swan. One year Oenghus also became a swan and together they flew off to his palace, Brugh na Bóinne in County Meath. In *The Children of Lir* the jealous stepmother uses a magic wand to change the king's four children into swans for nine hundred years. Irish poets, like the shamans of Siberia and North America, had cloaks of bird feathers. They could transform situations with words. Living in the three elements of air, earth and water, the swan was most versatile. It could communicate between worlds, and between person and creature. In Celtic belief a swan should not be harmed because it might embody a loved one's soul.

Many old Welsh stories have survived in an oral tradition until recent centuries. In Whitmore Bay on Barry Island, Glamorgan, a young farmer was said to have seen a beautiful swan alighting on rocks. There she put aside her feathers and wings, assumed the shape of a lovely maiden, bathed, then resumed her swan shape and flew away. After watching her several times the farmer laid in wait and seized her garments while she was bathing. When she came out of the water she begged him to return her wings but he refused. She succumbed to marrying him and for three years was faithful. Her husband kept her wings and feathers locked in an oaken chest, which one day he carelessly left open. Seizing her opportunity, she donned her swan's garment and flew away. He returned home in time to see his swan-wife disappearing into the sunset, crying a plaintive farewell. Grief-stricken, he pined away, dying a few months later.

That story was well known in the early part of the nineteenth century. At that time it was only possible to reach Barry Island when the tide was out. Two young wildfowlers became so engrossed in their sport on Whitmore Bay that they were cut off by the tide and unable to return to the mainland. Waiting for the tide to turn, they explored the rocks, where they saw two swans, which changed into beautiful maidens. In keeping with the folklore, the fowlers stole their garments and forced the maidens to marry them. Their children were conspicuous by their swan-shaped necks. Unfortunately one of the wives was run over by a wagon and killed. When folk rushed to her aid she assumed her swan-shape and flew away. After seven years of happy marriage, the other husband was unwise enough to throw out the swan garment, which she found and donned. Within minutes she flew away. In another Welsh tale a maiden called Grassi (Grace) was the keeper of a well in Caernarvonshire. Her duty was to open the door of the well and close it when folk had drawn enough water. One day she forgot to shut the door and the waters overflowed, forming a lake. For this neglect she was changed into a swan, haunting the lake for over three hundred years and uttering a regular plaintive cry in the small hours. The lonely lake is now the home of swans and her ghost, dressed in a soft white silk gown, is said to walk round a nearby house, where servants refused to stay because of her haunting.

Metamorphosis can be achieved without stealing magical covering, through performing sympathetic magic. Thus, believing in affinity between actions, women in a medicine dance among the Ogala Sioux Indians imitated the peculiar call of the female swan. Discussing the evolution of kings in *The Golden Bough*, Sir James Frazer records:

> Formerly it was customary to bury the chorion under the threshold, where the mother stepped over it daily when she rose from bed . . . If the chorion was thus treated, the man had in after life a guardian spirit in the shape of a bear, an eagle, a wolf, an ox, or a boar . . . while those of beautiful women appeared as swans.[5]

One of the romantic legends about the foundation of Japan is based on eighth-century history books. The hero, son of Emperor Keiko, twelfth in the imperial lineage, was ordered by his father to leave the capital, Yamato, to go and fight the tribes in southern and eastern Japan who refused to obey him. Recognizing the prince as the country's most outstanding practitioner of martial arts, the chief of a surrendering tribe gave him the honorary title of Yamato-takeruno-mikoto, by which he was henceforth known. Success on the battlefield, though, was mirrored by tragedy at home. Prince Yamato-takeru lost his beloved wife and himself suffered a fatal illness. He was buried in a mausoleum but onlookers saw a big white bird fly from the tomb. Finding the tomb empty, they followed the swan to open ground near the capital, where it displayed its beautiful white tail like the bottom of court robes before disappearing from sight. The area, named Habikino ('Wing-trailing field') after the event, became the site of imperial tombs, numbering some one hundred.

In China it was the tears of the first empress of the Qin dynasty that made a swan lake. To create a healthy environment in which he could live long the emperor arranged for part of the sea to be filled in and a bridge built. On hearing the gong the empress was to bring meals for the workmen. One day rampant dung beetles sounded the gong early, at which command the empress hurried to send meals. Angry that the empress had disobeyed him, the harsh emperor killed her. She cried a river, Tears Lake. In answer to people's prayers to bring her pure soul back to earth, flocks of swans fell from the sky to live on the lake.

A rich man who died in Thailand was reborn as a golden swan in heaven, where he lived contentedly on the Heavenly Lake. Looking down to earth, he saw that his widow was reduced to abject poverty so he flew down and made her an offer she could not refuse: 'Pluck one of my golden feathers and sell it in the city.' The sale was enough to pay for all she needed. Daily visits by her former husband kept her in comfort, but she became greedy. One day, on receiving the usual offer, she seized her swan-husband and quickly plucked out all his feathers, whereupon all the feathers turned white. The swan flew away, never to return. According to a tribe in Victoria, Australia, black swans are men who took refuge on a mountain during a flood and turned into black swans at the moment the water reached their feet.

Drawing on Russian folklore, Pushkin (1799–1837) retold in verse *The Tale of Tsar Saltan* in which the tsarevitch saves a swan who turns into a princess and becomes his bride, to the delight of his father, from whom he had been taken with his mother by her envious sisters. Another Slav tale, *Sweet Mikhail Ivanovich the Rover*, begins with Mikhail about to shoot a swan, but the bird warns him that the killing will bring him ill fortune for evermore. On landing the swan turns into a beautiful maiden. When he tries to kiss her she again has to warn him. She is an infidel, but there is a possibility of salvation. If he takes her to the holy city of Kiev she could be received into the church and thus be free to marry him.

A cautionary tale about a knight courting two sisters 'by the North Sea shore' is told in the doleful Scottish folk song 'Cruel Sister'. Not surprisingly, jealousy took a hand. The elder, darker sister threw the younger off the cliffs. 'And there she floated like a swan / The salt sea bore her body on / Fa la la la . . .' The maiden's body floated on to land, where passing minstrels found it and made a harp of her breastbone. Taken to the court where the elder sister and her knight are being married, the harp sings its accusation: 'In terror sits the black-haired bride.'

The celebrated male European legend is the knight of the swan, the French *Chevalier au cygne*. Well known by the end of the twelfth century, the legend relates how at the court of Emperor Otto the Duchess of Bouillon was pleading for justice against Saxon Duke Renier, who had made serious allegations against her. When she was in sore need of a champion to prove her innocence in single combat an unknown knight suddenly appeared in a skiff drawn by a swan. As a reward for defeating her opponent the knight of the swan married her daughter Beatris but on condition that she must never ask his name or origin. After seven years of marriage Beatris broke this condition and the unknown knight left her. Their daughter Ida became the mother of Godfrey of Bouillon, a leader of the First Crusade (1095–9), giving his house a supernatural origin.

The better-known German version is about Lohengrin, who appears at the end of *minnesinger* Wolfram von Eschenbach's chivalric poem *Parzival* about the Holy Grail (*c.* 1210), as the deliverer of Elsa, Princess of Brabant, from an unwanted suitor. He arrives in Antwerp in a skiff drawn by a swan, champions and marries Elsa on condition of anonymity. On their marriage night, by his vows to the Holy Grail, he is obliged to disclose his identity and disappears. Before the returning swan takes him away Lohengrin transforms Elsa's brother from swan back to human form. In honour of the *Schwanritter* legend in 1440, Frederick II of Brandenburg founded his 'Order of the Swan', first in Brandenburg and later in Cleves. The badge of the Order was a silver swan surmounted by an image of the Virgin Mary.

Anne of Cleves, daughter of the Duke of Cleves, arrived in England to become the fourth wife of Henry VIII in 1540, but after six months the marriage was declared void on the grounds of non-consummation. A popular figure from Flanders adapting to English ways, she remained in England, where she saw the 'White Swan' more widely adopted as a public house sign. The Order died out in the sixteenth century, not being revived until 1843 by Frederick William IV of Prussia. Wagner's romantic opera *Lohengrin* was first produced in Weimar in 1850, Wolfram's thirteenth-century epic poem being the source of the libretto and the Schwanenburg in Cleves the hero's eleventh-century castle. Legends are long-lived.

They survived partly through translation. For instance the Elizabethan printer Robert Copland (*fl.* 1505–1547) translated *The Knight of the Swan* from the French (1512). By this time the Middle Ages were over and the spirit of knight errantry with them. It was to be another century before Cervantes administered the apparent death blow to the romances of chivalry in *Don Quixote*. It would take another madman, Ludwig II of Bavaria, to give them a new lease of life in architecture and opera.

Short-lived was the operatic career of Walter Ullmann (1910–83). As a young student in Vienna he worked as an extra in opera. In a performance of *Lohengrin* he was fascinated by the way in which the swan glided on to the stage. Leaning over too far to examine the mechanism that propelled it, he lost his warrior's helmet and wig, which jammed the rails on which the swan was moving. The performance and Ullmann's operatic career both ended abruptly. His future was as a leading historian of the Middle Ages.

Although we have no written evidence for the origins of legends they can be traced by archaeological finds with some reasonable speculation on their significance. The swan was a cult bird in the European Bronze Age, from the second millennium BC into the Iron Age. It appears to be connected with solar cults and sacred thermal waters. Several votive models of carriages drawn by swans or in which the birds sat have survived. Probably the small chariots were models for real vehicles in which the image of the god, priest-king or swan-knight would have sat. Live birds may have accompanied the procession. In legends they are spoken of as flying overhead. Other important physical evidence consists of bronze swan heads, often with rings for chains under the beaks, in the supernatural metals gold and silver.

Pagan legends were handed down, memories modified and modified again when literate clerics came to write them down.

With the coming of Christianity, it was not difficult for the church to adopt the concepts associated with the bird, especially the transformation from the material to the supernatural world, which applied to both male and female. People could change or be changed for the better. The swan-knight was a role model of selfless service and the beauty and purity of the white swan was a symbol of the soul in a state of grace. In the Middle Ages, a high point of Christian faith, people took oaths upon the swan. Thus, on his investiture as a knight, King Edward I (*reg.* 1272–1307) swore an oath on two swans decorated with gold nets. His oath that he would conquer Scotland was never fulfilled. His jousting grandson, Edward III, took as his motto 'Hey, hey, the white Swan, / By Goddës love I am they man'. In his 50-year reign (1327–77) he did achieve an improvement in the status of the monarchy. Ambitious, he attempted to force his rule on Scotland and began the Hundred Years' War by laying claim to the French throne. As the swan's symbolic history demonstrates, transformation of whatever kind is about having aspirations, which may or may not be fulfilled.

4 In History

The earliest representations of swans date from before 4,500 BCE. For example, a few Mesolithic animal sculptures, including representations of swans, carved in amber have been unearthed in southern Scandinavia. During the second millennium BCE more representations occur in widely differing places, for instance in rock drawings at Lake Onega, Finland, and as a Babylonian unit of weight, the mina, possibly the first of all known weights. Units were not consistent in weight, examples varying from 640 grams (23 ounces) to 978 grams (34 ounces). Multiple units have been found, e.g. 5 minas in the shape of a duck and 30 minas in the form of a swan.[1]

Towards the end of the first millennium BCE the bird occurs as a decorative element. At the height of Roman naval power, when the prow of a ship was developed as a ramming and piercing weapon, the sternpost became the focus of decoration. Fashioned to sweep high in a graceful curve, it terminated in a figure such as the gilded head of a swan.[2] A round wooden table, found in Egypt, was decorated with swans' heads, their graceful necks rising from a band of acanthus foliage.[3]

The ubiquity of swans is evident from place names. Swan hills, islands, lakes and rivers are found in Australia, Canada and the United States. For example, in 1697 the explorer Willem de Vlamingh named an ephemeral river in south-western Australia Swan River for the black swans found in its lower

The eighteen swan bells in Perth, Western Australia, are housed in a bell tower built for the millennium. External louvres in the form of swans' wings both muffle and direct the sound of the bells, twelve of which were donated by St Martin-in the-Fields, London, to mark the bicentenary of Australia in 1988.

reaches. It was one of the zoological novelties described and illustrated by George Shaw in his *Naturalist's Miscellany*, produced in 24 volumes (1789–1813). In 1829, when the first settlers came to what are the present sites of Fremantle and Perth, the

area became known as Swan River Colony. Off the coast a small tree in the cypress family growing on Rottnest and other islands in the Indian Ocean is sometimes called Swan River Pine. Swan Hill, over in northern Victoria, was given its name in the 1830s by another explorer, Thomas Mitchell, who was kept awake by the call of the swans. Recognizing its affinity to the Swan of Avon, the city now stages an annual Shakespearean festival. Although the bird can be found on wetlands throughout the country, including Tasmania, it represents Western Australia on the Australian coat of arms. On the emblem of the capital, Canberra, it is a symbol of the Aboriginal people while the white swan represents Australians of European ancestry.

In Britain there are combinations such as Swanbourne, a place frequented by swans, and Swanmore, a low-lying marshy habitat. On the face of it the village of Swanland in the East Riding of Yorkshire, near the estuary of the River Humber, is another such combination. The first element is more likely to be an Old Scandinavian personal name, which occurs in Iceland

and as a nickname in Norway.[4] 'Swan' is also a version of 'swain', a boy or servant, or an occupational name meaning a herdsman, swineherd or peasant. Not all word combinations in English place names refer to the bird.

Swanendael, the first Dutch settlement in what became the US state of Delaware, means Valley of the Swans. German *Schwan* combines with suffixes such as *berg* (hill), *dorf* (village), *gau* (district), *heim* (home). *Schwanseepark* means Swan Lake Park. The family estate of Josef Goebbels, Hitler's Minister of Public Enlightenment and Propaganda, was *Schwanenwerder*, Swans' Island. One suggestion for the origin of Valenciennes in northern France is *Val des cygnes* (Valley of the Swans); there is a swan on the civic coat of arms. In Paris *Allée des Cygnes* is an artificial island in the Seine, a tree-lined walk at the western end of which is a bronze scale replica of the Statue of Liberty, a gift from the Parisian community in the United States in 1885 in return for the original presented by France to New York the previous year. St Petersburg has a Swan Canal by the French-inspired Summer Gardens.

The best known work of John Leland, Henry VIII's antiquary who made an itinerary of England, is a river poem *Cygnea Cantio* (1545), a Latin account of thirteen swans making their way down the Thames from Oxfordshire to the estuary. At the time the river was relatively pure. Holinshed, a contemporary chronicler, recorded in 1577 'fat and sweet salmons [are] taken' and 'the water ittselfe is very cleare' with 'infinit number of swans daile to be seenee'.[5] In *Travels in England During the Reign of Queen Elizabeth* (1612) the German traveller Paul Hentzen noted ' Near this place [Parliament at Westminster] are seen an immense number of swans, who wander up and down the river for some miles, in great security; nobody daring to molest, much less kill any of them, under penalty of considerable fine.'[6] The English traveller Fynes Moryson noted in his voluminous work *An Itinerary* (1617), 'England abounds with all kinds of fowl as well of the sea as of the land, and hath more tame swans swimming in the rivers, than I did see in any other part.'[7] Their presence led to landmark names.

There was a Swan Tavern at Charing Cross and another, frequented by Samuel Pepys, stood near the Thames at Chelsea, giving its name to Swan Walk. The Old Swan was a famous City tavern at the river end of Swan Lane. Boat passengers not wanting to risk the rapids under London Bridge disembarked at Old Swan Stairs. The watermen's half-hour race for Doggett's Coat and Badge, instituted to mark the accession of George I in 1715, was run from The Old Swan, London Bridge, to the Old Swan at Chelsea. Along the river were Swan inns in Arundel Street, at Battersea, Hungerford Stairs and Lambeth. In Southwark was the 3,000-capacity Swan Theatre, like the neighbouring Globe an Elizabethan structure. 'Swan' was the name of one of the small supply ships accompanying Sir Francis Drake on his voyage round the world in 1577–80.

Often signs were not direct depictions of the bird, but heraldic. Heraldry was a visual shorthand. A coat of arms, with its colourfully embroidered badge and crest, was originally worn over a knight's armour to distinguish a leader, especially in the heat of battle. Stewards of a mediaeval jousting tournament chose a clearly distinguishable bird or beast as an emblem, the different ranks of the nobility being indicated by the type of metal finish, gold, silver and a mixture of gilt and silver. For retainers livery badges with pins were cast in pewter. In an illiterate society an illustration immediately gave an identity to an inn. A 1393 statute of King Richard II made it compulsory for every inn in England to display a sign.

His usurper successor, Henry IV (1399–1413), took as his first wife Lady Mary de Bohun, whose family claimed descent from

the Knight of the Swan. The king included a swan as a supporter in his coat of arms, a bird that was often copied in inn signs. The swan was the badge of the Bohuns, the earls of Chichester, Stafford and other families. It was in the crest of Sir Richard Charleton, who was killed on the Yorkist side at the Battle of Bosworth, 1485. On the arms of the Vintners' Company a cob and pen stand as supporters. When the Poulters' Company was granted arms in 1634 swans figured with cranes, later to be replaced by hens and turkeys.

In heraldry the bird is shown in various positions: 'close' its wings are folded to its body; 'couchant' it rests on its belly with its head up; 'gorged' it has a collar round its neck to which is attached a chain, referring to the legend of the Swan Knight travelling in a boat drawn by swans; 'issuant' with its upper half visible, rising from a base; 'regardant' it is looking backward; 'rising' or, rarely, 'rousant' it is getting ready for flight. It appears thus twice on a coat of arms brought to Poland from Denmark by Piotr Dunin in 1124, enduring to this day in many families bearing the name Dunin. Most widely used in the

Cracow and Sandomierz regions of southern Poland, it was also adopted by Lithuanian families following the union of the Grand Duchy of Lithuania and the kingdom of Poland in 1386. Altogether some 150 families there used the swan crest.

Behind most coats of arms there is usually a mixture of legend, historical fact and fiction summed up in the word tradition. Selby Abbey, for instance, a Norman foundation established in Yorkshire soon after the Conquest of 1066, has as its coat of arms three swans. Its origin is said to be in fifth-century France, where from 418 to 448 nobleman and soldier St Germanus was bishop of Auxerre, 100 miles south-east of Paris. Twice he visited Britain to combat Pelagian heresy. Over 600 years after his death he appeared one night in a vision at Auxerre Abbey to a monk, Benedict, instructing him to go to Selby and build an abbey. Defying opposition from his abbot and fellow monks, Benedict left Auxerre under cover of darkness, taking with him the middle finger of St Germanus's right hand, a precious relic.

At first he went to Salisbury, Wiltshire, but Germanus redirected him to the lonely site of Selby, Yorkshire. Sailing up the River Ouse, Benedict recognized the site from a scene in his vision, confirmed when three swans alighted on the river, which he took as a sign of the Holy Trinity. On the bank under a great oak he set up a wooden cross as a marker. William the Conqueror was so impressed in about 1069 by the piety of Benedict that he ordered the immediate foundation of a monastery, a counterpart to that he had ordered at Battle after his 1066 victory at Hastings. The rebel monk Benedict became the first abbot of the new Benedictine monastery.[8] The medieval arms of three swans can be seen in the Bishop of Selby's stall on the north side of the choir in York Minster and in the town of Selby. As a permanent memorial of the millennium the Masonic lodge of St Germain no. 566

The symbol of Selby Civic Society, Yorkshire, derives from Benedict's sighting of three swans, which he took to represent the Holy Trinity and the site of his future monastery.

This swan vignette for illustrations to *Le Morte d'Arthur* are in the typical style of Aubrey Beardsley (1872–1898).

undertook, with the support of over 90 other lodges in the province, the restoration of the St William window in York Minster using the crest of three swans it had adopted.

An earlier saint having an association with York was bishop Paulinus, one of the second band of missionaries sent from Rome to England in 601. A tall, dark man of venerable and awe-inspiring appearance, he contributed to the peace and order during the last years of the reign of King Edwin of Northumbria (617–633). When Paulinus, bishop of Rochester, died in 644 his soul was reported to have been seen ascending to Heaven 'in the form of an exceedingly beautiful great white bird, like a swan'. Carried aloft by two silver swans was the soul of St Modwenna, venerated at Burton-upon-Trent, Staffordshire, where from about the tenth century she was the patron saint of the wells from which water for the brewing industry was drawn.

Another mediaeval saint associated with a swan was Hugh of Lincoln (*c.* 1135–1200). Although he described himself as 'peppery', he had the ability to win the respect of royalty, Jews and the whooper swan he met at the episcopal manor in Stowe. As if predestined, the graceful creature, with gold glistering about its head and neck, arrived at the same time as the bird-loving bishop, to whom it was introduced. Sensing a friend, it accepted a piece of bread from his hand and became an immediate pet. Occasionally it would insinuate its head up Hugh's long sleeve as though it wanted to whisper in his ear. It could also be fiercely protective, rising with arched wings to keep 'intruders' at bay. Intruders of its own species were similarly warned off the manorial waters, with the exception of a pen that was only a companion. They did not breed. When Hugh returned from diocesan visits the swan would fly excitedly along the water,

Mourning swans at the foot of the 14th-century effigy of Margaret de Bohun in Exeter Cathedral.

land and walk either to the hall or the outer gate in welcome. The exception was the bishop's last visit not long before his death. As if gifted with prophecy, the bird did not come out in welcome and was with difficulty coaxed into his room. After Hugh's death it did not pine away.[9]

Affinity to swans was not confined to saints. There is a romantic legend, probably dating from the nineteenth century, on the persistence of swans on the Minnewater in the medieval town of Bruges in the Austrian Netherlands. In 1488 the inhabitants of the town executed Pieter Lanchals, an administrator appointed by Maximilian of Austria. Lanchals means long neck and his family coat of arms featured a white swan. According to the legend, Maximilian punished Bruges by ordering its citizens to keep swans on their lakes and canals for ever.[10] Just before being burned at the stake for heresy in 1415 the Czech religious

A solitary swan in a fresco in the Pope's wardrobe at the Papal Palace, Avignon, could have been a rare example of purity during the 14th-century exile of the Papacy from Rome. Dominated by France, the papal court was notorious for its splendour and luxury.

Jan Guldenmundt (*d.* 1560) told the story of two Protestant reformers, Jan Hus and Martin Luther, in this undated woodcut with differing swans at the foot. Hus was burned at the stake in 1415; the swan became Luther's symbol.

reformer Jan Hus wrote from his prison cell 'Today you are roasting a lean goose [Hus is the Czech word for goose]; however, from my ashes in a hundred years a swan will ascend that you cannot roast – you will have to listen to him.' In 1517 Martin Luther, the German leader of the Protestant Reformation, nailed his 95 theses on the door of the castle church in Wittenberg. From there through preaching and writing his doctrines spread. After his death in 1546 Luther, who regarded himself as a swan come to reform the Church, was often portrayed with a swan in sculptures, paintings, woodcuts, engravings, hymnals and commemorative coins. Instead of roosters and crosses on weather vanes swans were to be seen on Lutheran church steeples and schools in Northern Germany and the Netherlands.[11]

During the Counter Reformation in England, the reign of Queen Mary (1553–8), one of more than 300 Protestants from all walks of life burned at the stake was nineteen-year-old William Hunter, who maintained 'his right to search the scriptures and in all matters of faith and practice to follow their sole guidance'. Those words appeared on an obelisk erected by public subscription in 1861 on the site of his martyrdom in Brentwood, Essex. On its base is inscribed 'He being dead yet speaketh'. This is doubly appropriate in that his ghost haunts The Swan Inn where he was imprisoned before his final ordeal. Resentful of his treatment, his silent shade continued to make the mischief of a poltergeist.[12]

Almost four centuries later swans figured in deliverance from sectarian conflict. The poet Oliver St John Gogarty (1878–1957), appointed a senator of the newly created Irish Free State in 1922, was kidnapped by armed men from his house in Dublin between seven and eight in the evening, hurried into a motor, and driven to a deserted house on the banks of the Liffey. Fellow poet W. B. Yeats takes up the story:

> As he was not blindfolded it seemed unlikely that he would return. 'Death by shooting is a very good death' said one of the armed men. 'Isn't it a fine thing to die to a flash' said another armed man. 'Have we any chance of a Republic, Senator?' said a third. They sent a man to report on their success and while waiting his return Oliver Gogarty played bodily feebleness that they might relax their care . . . He saw his moment, plunged into the river and escaped into the darkness, not hearing in the

roar of flooded water the shots fired at random. Forced
for his safety to leave Ireland for a time, he practised his
profession in London . . . He telephoned me at the Savile
Club to know where he could buy two swans. Up to his
neck in its ice cold water he had promised two swans to
the Liffey if permitted to land in safety. I made inquiries
and was able to report in a couple of days that there were
certainly swans for sale at a well-known English country
house and probably at the Zoological Gardens.[13]

In 1923 *An Offering of Swans*, a collection of poems by Gogarty,
was published in Dublin with a preface by Yeats, from which
the above account is taken. The final poem in the short collection was 'To the Liffey with the Swans':

Keep you these calm and lovely things,
And float them on your clearest water;
For one would not disgrace a King's
Transformed beloved and buoyant daughter.
And with her goes this sprightly swan,
A bird of more than royal feather
With alban beauty clothed upon:
O keep them fair and well together!

As fair as was that doubled Bird
By love of Leda so besotten,
That she was all with wonder stirred:
And the Twin Sportsmen were begotten!

Almost fifty years later there was a peace offering on a grander
scale when, after twenty years of hostility, President Nixon was
going to meet the ageing Chairman Mao Zedong and establish

normal relations with China. Helen Boehm, head of a porcelain firm, had suggested to the president that a new symbol was needed for a bird of peace for the world as the dove was somewhat tarnished and not all countries recognized it. He gave her the job. After rejecting various suggestions

> Finally we unanimously agreed that the bird would be the mute swan, representing serenity and purity, a bird that had been associated with peace throughout history and in mythology. The mute swan's range is worldwide . . . Perhaps its most important characteristic is that it speaks with a soft voice.[14]

A pair of swans took two years and ten tons of plaster to make. Sixty thousand feathered barbs had to be detailed on the model. Three young cygnets and lily pads were added to the ground base. It was presented as one of Nixon's gifts to the people of China on his visit in February 1972, an elegant element in détente.

Swans are a natural motif for designers. The earliest known carving by Caius Cibber (1630–1700), a sculptor to Charles II, is the swan mantelpiece of c. 1656 in the high room at Lamport Hall, Northamptonshire, designed by John Webb. As a piece of decoration the swan fitted easily into the following century, an age of elegance. Louis XV, king of France 1715–74, had in his extravagance at the Palace of Versailles a pair of candelabra with Dresden figures of swans. They inspired American poet Marianne Moore (1887–1972) to write a poem 'No Swan So Fine', beginning

> 'No water so still as the
> dead fountains of Versailles.' No swan,
> with swart blind look askance
> and gondoliering legs, so fine

as the chintz china one with fawn-
brown eyes and toothed gold
collar on to show whose bird it was.

The swan service was a set of porcelain tableware made at the
Meissen factory between 1737 and 1741. Comprising 2,200 pieces,
the dinner service was made to the order of Augustus III, Elector
of Saxony, for presentation to the recently married director of
the factory Count von Brühl and Countess Kolowrat-Krakowski.
In the Rococo style, the theme of the *Schwanengeschirr* was
water, which may have been inspired by the count's name,
which means swampy meadow or marshy ground. The design

This item of
Meissen swan
service dates
from *c*. 1730.

includes swans, dolphins and nereids. A swan easily served as a sauce boat. Later one of the designers, the sculptor J. J. Kändler (1706–1775), made a Meissen figure of a swan on a waterweed mound base. A German silver swan also made an elegant centrepiece for a table.

The swan-neck handle was a curved, hanging brass handle introduced in the early 1760s on the drawers of case furniture such as chests of drawers and bureaux. Swan-neck pediments, used for instance by Thomas Chippendale (1718–1779) in the design of a library bookcase, were formed of two s-shaped curves with perhaps an urn between them. The design was also used on longcase (American tallcase) clocks, popularly known as grandfather clocks. A rainwater pipe connecting a gutter to a downpipe is an outside example of a swan-neck.

According to Sheraton's *Cabinet Dictionary* (1803), swan-neck hinges were a kind of pin-hinge, smaller versions of the wrought iron cock's head used in the previous century. They avoided the disagreeable appearance of the knockle [knuckle] of common but-hinges [*sic*] on the external part of neatly finished work. These are let into the ends of doors so as to bring the centre of the pin even with the front, otherwise it will not clear in turning, and that the projecting strap which has the pin may be behind. It is let into the top and bottom of the carcase into which the door shuts, and the door ends slip into the other strap of the hinge which has not the pin.

A swan-neck spout was long and thin, with an s-shaped curve in the form of a swan's neck. A swan cup was a type of coffee cup made at Sèvres in the first decade of the nineteenth century in the form of a swan. Its curved-down neck was the handle. The inside of the cup and the well of the oval saucer on which it stood were gilded. In the mid-nineteenth century swans were made in Staffordshire porcelain and later in Goss china. The head of the bird, sometimes the whole bird, also figured as the tops of canes and cameo glass scent bottles, its fine detail later making them an antique collector's item.

In the twentieth century, which periodically had its styles of elegance, the swan also featured. When Liza, W. Somerset Maugham's daughter, married Vincent Paravicini, son of the Swiss Minister to England, in 1936, the *New York Times* and the *Daily Express* noted: 'the wedding presents stood the test of elegance and included pale-blue sheets embroidered with white swans, given by Lady Jowitt.'[15] In 1951, during the official Festival of Britain holiday, the artist John Ward drew fellow artist Geraldine Lawrence breakfasting in her swan-shaped bed at home among works by the French artist Raoul Dufy (1877–1953).[16] The Swan was the name the twentieth-century Danish designer Arne Jacobsen gave to a chair, one of a pair he produced in 1958, the other being The Egg.

Swan curiosities were not new. Late fourteenth-century mazers, drinking bowls, instead of the usual boss in the bottom have a silver-gilt swan with a down-turned neck. By means of a pillar with a hollow tube the swan appears to be drinking liquid poured into the bowl. Of the surviving examples, one is owned by Corpus Christi College, Cambridge, and four are recorded in Kent hospitals, one in St James's, Canterbury, and three in the nearby village of Harbledown.

A 1773 lifesize silver swan automaton is now in the Bowes Museum, Barnard Castle, County Durham. The bird appears to float on 'water' simulated by rotating glass rods. Hidden machinery, including chains running up the slender neck and a pair of spring-operated tongs, makes the neck bend down and give the impression of catching a fish in the 'water'. Mark Twain saw it at the Paris Exposition 1867 and recorded the experience in *Innocents Abroad* (1869), a travel book based on letters he wrote to US newspapers:

> I watched a Silver Swan which had a living grace about his movements and a living intelligence in his eyes – watched him swimming about as comfortable as unconcernedly as if he had been born in a morass instead of a jeweller's shop – watched him seize a silver fish from under the water and hold his head and go through all the customary and elaborate motions of swallowing it . . .

In the mid-eighteenth century there was a fascination for conjuring entertainments. Many of these were based on magnets and mechanisms used by the great French conjuror Comus. Sir Francis Delaval, a rake, was reputed to have ruined the act of conjuror Philip Breslau at the Haymarket Theatre, London, by wielding in the audience his own powerful magnet. This made it impossible for the conjuror to control the movements of his magnetically driven 'learned little swan, which was supposed to pick out letters from a bowl in response to questions'.[17]

A tongue-twister nursery rhyme was popular, certainly in the nineteenth century:

Swan swam over the sea,
Swim, swan, swim!
Swan swam back again,
Well swam swan.

A person much associated with curiosities is 'Mad King' Ludwig II of Bavaria (1845–1886). During the spring of 1867 Ludwig visited the Wartburg, near Eisenach in Thuringia, where in the minstrels' hall Wagner had set the singing contest in *Tannhäuser*. The setting was the inspiration for Schloss Neuschwanstein, built between 1869 and 1886 south of Munich, a fantastic structure with swan motifs such as a solid silver tap spouting water from its beak in Ludwig's bedroom. His castle was intended to be a shrine to Lohengrin, Tannhäuser, Parsifal and the knights of medieval German chivalry. In a letter to Richard Wagner dated 13 May 1868 Ludwig stated his intention

to rebuild the ancient castle ruins of Hohenschwangau in the genuine style of the old German knights' castles . . . This castle will be in every respect more beautiful and comfortable than the lower-lying Hohenschwangau, which is yearly profaned by my mother's 'prose'. The outraged gods will take their revenge and sojourn with us on the steep summit, fanned by celestial breezes.

The mad King Ludwig II with swans in the Venus Grotto at his Lindenhof castle.

In the nineteenth century the cultural shift was towards music. Among the 145 songs Franz Schubert, the greatest exponent of German *Lieder*, composed in 1815, his most productive year, was 'Schwanengesang' (Swansong). The title in fact comprised fourteen songs, including poems by Heine, Rellstab and Seidl, published posthumously in 1895. Much of the inspiration was from the past. Tchaikovsky (1840–1893) admired Wagner and reviewed his concerts, including the first Bayreuth Festival (1876). He particularly admired *Lohengrin*, the story of the swan-prince hero who arrives on a magical swan boat. Doubtless Tchaikovsky would have been familiar with legends of swan maidens and other folk tales in which the bird is a symbol of womanhood at its purest. Fantasized supernatural creatures lent themselves to abstract choreography for the corps de ballet. To amuse his sister's children he wrote a little ballet *The Lake of the Swans*. Four years later, in 1875, he was commissioned to write a score for *Swan Lake* for the sum of 800 roubles. After its Moscow première in 1877 it had a chequered history, with choreographers not doing justice to the music, which admittedly included passages composed for previous operatic projects. It was not until 1895, two years after Tchaikovsky's death, that what is now regarded as the standard version, a combination of graceful movement and technical precision by Pepita and his assistant Ivanov, received its première at the Mariinsky Theatre in St Petersburg. The complete ballet and the familiar suite from it were only published posthumously.

The story of Prince Siegfried's love for Odette was reworked in the 1994 animated film *The Swan Princess*. A few feathers were ruffled at the 2001 Oscar ceremonies, a fashion parade as much as an awards occasion, when Icelandic pop star Björk appeared in a *Swan Lake* tutu, complete with billed head, stitched on to a flesh-coloured bodysuit. At the beginning of the twenty-first century Australian Dance Theatre radically reworked *Swan Lake* for the stage as *Birdbrain*, drawing on elements of classical ballet, contemporary dance, breakdance, yoga, contortionism and gymnastics. So popular has the ballet been that

Even the curtains in Ludwig II's castle Neuschwanstein had a swan design.

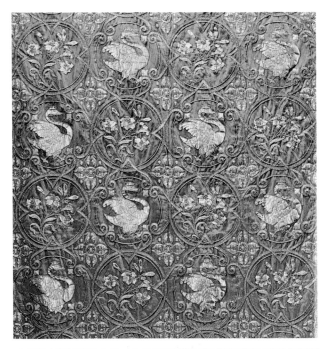

A 1997 production of *Swan Lake*.

Matthew Bourne's
acclaimed all-male
production of
Swan Lake at
Sadlers Wells,
London, 2004.

Björk in swan
dress at the
75th anniversary
celebration of
the Oscars in
Hollywood,
March 2001.

it has entered rhyming slang: Swan Lake, shortened to swan, equals cake.

The Finnish composer Jean Sibelius (1865–1957) drew upon an old Finnish epic, the *Kalevala*, in which the bird swims the river separating the living from the dead, for what became one of his most popular works, the tone poem *The Swan of Tuonela* (1893). Originally conceived as the prelude to an opera *The Burning of the Boat*,[18] the piece remained alone when the opera was abandoned. This probably followed Sibelius's visit to Bayreuth in 1894, where he witnessed the magnitude of Wagner's achievement. One of the Norwegian folk songs of Edvard Grieg (1843–1907) was entitled 'The Swan'. 'Le Cygne' was the exception French composer Saint-Saëns made when he forbade performances during his lifetime of *Le Carnival des Animaux* (1886), which he regarded as a private joke penned as a holiday relaxation.[19] Performed after the death of its short-lived composer Arthur Goring Thomas (1850–1892) was *The Swan and the Skylark* by the poet Felicia Hemans (1793–1835). The cantata was orchestrated by C. V. Stanford and performed at the Birmingham Festival in 1894.

In the twentieth century some musical groups have allied themselves with the musical bird. A hit for the acoustic duo T Rex in 1970 was Marc Bolan's hippie lyric beginning 'Ride a white swan like the people of the Beltane / Wear your hair long baby, can't go wrong'. It reached Number 2 and stayed for five months in the charts of the top 40 UK records. Some black gospel singers called themselves the Swan Silvertones.[20] Swan Song, named after one of five songs Led Zeppelin never recorded for commercial release, was the name of the band's own record label. In the 1980s The Swans – a band that was part of the New York underground – determined to stretch the bounds of musical cacophony with titles such as 'Greed', 'Holy Money', 'Raping a Slave' and 'Public Castration is a Good Idea'. The name would seem to be ironic.

Cygnus as the Latin name for the large constellation in the Milky Way dates from the mid-sixteenth century but the shape was known earlier. A crude but reasonably accurate representation of it appears, for instance, in *De cursu stellarum*, written by Gregory of Tours shortly after his consecration as a bishop in 573 and preserving vestiges of Greek and Roman astronomy. It appears in the Carolingian computational collection of 809, which soon formed part of anthologies of astronomical knowledge, including classical science and mythology. Among these were star catalogues, as they were commonly called, descriptions of the constellations taken from various ancient sources such as Pliny's *Natural History*. Not giving the position of the stars in any mathematical system of coordinates, they are qualitative descriptions of the constellations, noting the number of the stars in each part of the constellation and the general location of the brighter stars. In Cygnus the brightest star Deneb, meaning tail of the bird, is an Arabic form of the description by Ptolemy (*c.* AD 90–168), who was not the first observer. The stars in the constellation form a distinctive cross shape, giving it the alternative names of the Greater or Northern Cross, which is much larger than the Southern Cross, first recognized by the maritime explorers of the fifteenth and sixteenth centuries. It is divided by a dark lane of dust called the Cygnus Rift. Astronomically it is an interesting constellation, encompassing some fascinating objects: the brightest extragalactic radio source Cygnus A, believed to be two galaxies colliding; the small but strong x-Ray source Cygnus x-1, flickering on and off a thousand times a second, the likeliest candidate for a black hole of stellar mass; the brightest dwarf nova ss Cygni; the Veil Nebula, part of the Cygnus Loop, a large supernova remnant some 2,000

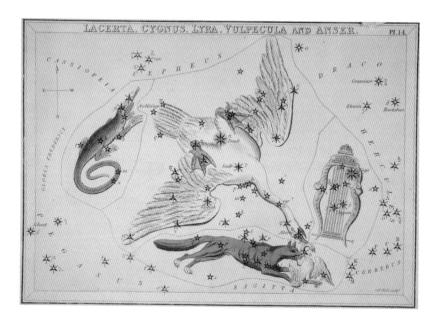

This hand-coloured etching by Sidney Hall of the constellations Cygnus, Lyra, Lacerta, Vulpecula and Anser (Swan, Lyre, Lizard, Fox and Goose) appeared in Jehoshaphat Aspin's *A Familiar Treaties on Astronomy* (1825).

light years away; and the North American Nebula. Albireo (Beta Cygni) has been called a sky showpiece double, its contrasting yellow and blue-green stars like a celestial traffic light.

Ever since the speculations of Ancient Greek scientists on the nature of light, opinion had been divided on whether it consisted of particles or waves. Newton described light as a stream of 'fiery particles'. Such was his reputation that this view tended to be accepted, though he himself doubted it following his observations of soap bubbles, which displayed on their surfaces an array of shifting colours, Newton's rings. Spacing between the rings depended upon the colour: blue rings were closer than red ones. Why? Nearly three-quarters of a century after Newton's death in 1727 a physician and physicist, Thomas Young, observed intersecting ripples set up by swans on the pond of Emmanuel College, Cambridge. Like Newton, Young thought on his observations continually. He outlined his train of reasoning:

It was in May, 1801, that I discovered, by reflecting on the beautiful experiments of Newton, a law which appears to me to account for a greater variety of interesting phenomena than any other optical principle that has yet been made known . . . Suppose a number of equal waves of water to move upon the surface of a stagnant lake, with a certain constant velocity, and to enter a narrow channel leading out of the lake; – suppose then another similar cause to have excited another equal series of waves, which arrive at the same channel, with the same velocity, and at the same time with the first . . . their effects will be combined . . . if the elevations of one series are so situated as to correspond to the depressions of the other, they must exactly fill up those depressions, and the surface of the water must remain smooth . . .

Now, I maintain that similar effects take place whenever two portions of light are thus mixed; and this I call the general law of the interference of light.[21]

Thomas Young demonstrated his support for the wave theory of light by a single source of light directed at two slits cut in a card, creating on a screen a series of light and dark lines, an interference pattern. Where the waves cancelled one another out the result was darkness; where they reinforced one another there was light. Thus Young explained the phenomena of the colours in soap bubbles, Newton's rings, a film of oil and polished mother-of-pearl. In each case there are two reflecting surfaces close together.

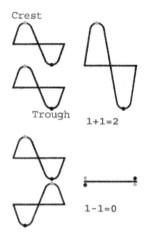

Crest

Trough $1+1=2$

$1-1=0$

Progress in another branch of science was furthered by swan-necks. Until the seventeenth century the prevailing view was that disease was caused by air that carried an element, a gas, fluid or some 'animalcule' that had the power to arouse life. In this miasma spontaneous generation took place. Experiments showed that this was not universally so, for example maggots in rotting flesh developed from eggs, but these observations were not generalized. By the mid-nineteenth century scientific opinion was divided between the Contagionists, who argued against the theory of spontaneous generation, and the Anti-Contagionists, who supported it.

Partly through his interest in solving problems with fermentation in the wine industry, the nineteenth-century French chemist Louis Pasteur wanted to find out where the microbes of putrefaction and disease came from and how they managed to multiply. 'If germs exist in atmosphere, could they not be arrested on their way?' The important thing was not to allow a liquid to come into contact with contaminated air. Having established that yeast, the classic fermenting agent used in making alcohol, was not a chemical but a microbe, Pasteur used sugared yeast-water as a liquid, which he boiled. His initial flasks were simple upright ones. Air, sterilized by being passed through a red-hot platinum tube and thus free from contamination, was introduced into the flasks. Sealed flasks showed no contamination even after a lengthy period of storage whereas the unsealed flasks left open to the atmosphere putrefied within a matter of days. He repeated the experiments in different locations at different heights, from the cellars of the Observatory of Paris to Mer de Glace in the Alps. Results varied according to sealed/unsealed flasks and the relative purity of the air.

The convincing demonstration that sterile air did not contain particles capable of generating life came from Pasteur's redesigned flask. Instead of an upright flask he used ones with a swan-neck in various shaped extensions but with only a one or two-millimetre opening. Some he filled with a boiled solution, others unboiled. The results were soon obvious. Within a few days the unboiled flasks were covered with moulds whereas the boiled solutions remained sterile for months without any trace of microbes. When the boiled flasks were tipped on their sides so that the sterile solution came into contact with the curved section in the drawn-out neck moulds soon developed. Pasteur pointed out that 'sinuosities and inclinations' of the swan-necked flasks had trapped the dust carried in the air and protected the solution from being contaminated. His conclusion was that 'nothing in the air – whether oxygen or other gases, fluids, electricity, magnetism, ozone, or some unknown occult agent – was required for microbial life except the germs carried by atmospheric dusts'. It was a major advance in bacteriology. The notion that microbes caused diseases led to Lister's development of antiseptic surgery, Pasteur's work on rabies and Koch's isolation of the tuberculosis bacillus. Acceptance of the germ theory of disease directed attention to treatment and prevention. In time attention would turn to diseases in the swan itself.

5 Hazards

In his Swedish police procedural *Before the Frost* (2004) Henning Mankell conveys at the end of the first chapter the horror of murdering swans:

> He got up, took a can in each hand and splashed the swans with petrol. Before they had a chance to fly away, he spread what remained in each of the cans and set light to a clump of dried grass among the swans. The burning petrol caught one swan and then all of them. In their agony, their wings on fire, they tried to fly away over the lake, but one by one plunged into the water like fireballs. He tried to fix the sight and sound of them in his memory; both the burning, screeching birds in the air and the image of hissing, smoking wings as they crashed into the lake. Their dying screams sounded like broken trumpets, he thought.[1]

On the evidence of swan rescue centres, the greatest danger to swans is man's activities, illegal and perfectly legal. Vandals, immune to beauty, regard swans as targets, especially at moult time when they are unable to move far. Birds are living creatures, not inanimate targets for missiles. Weapons include air guns, bottles, bricks, stones, even crossbow bolts. If air gun or rifle pellets do not kill they can often put out eyes or damage the jaw, imperilling life. A swan hit in the neck may fall into the water, slowly drowning. Such deaths cause stress among members of the family, which often swim around the carcase. After vandals killed its mate a swan attacked sheep. There have been instances of loud fireworks making birds die of fright. Restrictions have been placed on the discharge of fireworks but repeated calls for the banning of air guns have fallen on deaf ears. Humans have to suffer before action is taken.

Determined egg collectors have no qualms about driving a pen off a nest by shooting or battering her. In common with other poaching offences, the penalty for stealing eggs is lighter than it was. Cruelty seems mindless. Deliberately polluting waters with tar and oil means a big clean-up operation in the waters and of the birds themselves in rescue centres. The RSPCA has had to destroy 60 swans after oil was deliberately emptied into a river. Paint has been thrown over plumage. A large brown stain, still hot, on a bird, was caused by coffee discharged by a fisherman from a Thermos to discourage interference with his sport.

Vandals leave evidence of their sick minds in various ways. Destroyed and empty nests mean that there will be fewer cygnets. Some people short of a Christmas dinner have been known to smother and wrestle a swan. The practice was alleged to have increased around the millennium with the 'flood' of asylum seekers and illegal immigrants. Thoughtless litter louts discard plastic bags, which can enmesh the head, causing suffocation. Broken glass injures feet and legs, sometimes causing loss of blood to the extent of the bird having to be put on a drip.

A larger danger is loss of habitat. It is easy to regard wetlands as wastelands that need reclaiming to become productive or useful. Concern is frequently expressed about drilling for that most necessary modern commodity, oil, in places like Alaska. Man also needs living space. A prime example is the expansion of

China's major financial and commercial centre Shanghai. At the mouth of the Yangtse, it is in a strategic position, attracting investment to the area, including Chongming Island. Here land, which has become more valuable with economic development, has been reclaimed from marshland. Although there is Chongming Dongtan Bird Protection Zone, a stopover for migrant birds flying between Siberia and China, Korea and Japan, far fewer swans visit it.

Some of man's activities cause intoxication and injury. Oil and, worse, chemical spills and pollution are too frequent an example. Sportsmen are also blamed, particularly anglers who leave lines, lures and hooks lying around. These get tangled during casting or snap when snagged. Silk line used to decay fairly quickly but nylon, being almost impervious to the effects of air,

Birds getting entangled in fishing line is an all too frequent occurrence.

An external sign
of a swallowed
fishing-hook is
a swollen neck.

water and bacteria, remains a hazard for a long time. In fly
fishing hooks tend to snag on bankside obstructions and vegetation; in coarse fishing most snag on underwater or marginal
vegetation. During the closed season for coarse fishing, March
to June, distress calls to swan sanctuaries are noticeably
reduced. An official of the National Animal Rescue Association
in Britain has described the suffering inflicted upon the nation's
birds as 'nothing short of the worst kind of vandalism'.

When fishing tackle is ingested during feeding birds suffer
lacerated beaks and throats and they can slowly starve to death.
Hooks can become embedded in the tongue. For instance, a Fire
Brigade has rescued a swan ensnared by fishing line and a huge
triple-hooked lure designed for catching pike. Barbs were deeply
embedded in the tongue, which the bird tried to dislodge by rubbing her beak on her neck, causing the other hooks on the lure
to slice into her neck. Completely tangled in the fishing line, the
bird was drifting helplessly in the river. Cuts may be infected to
the point where maggots occur. Entanglement in line can sever
wings and may necessitate amputation of a limb. It is not
always possible to stitch a wing back on to the body.

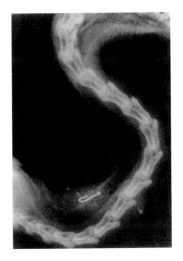

An x-ray reveals where a fishing barb is lodged.

Surgery is the only solution for removing a fishing barb.

Surgery, here on a damaged wing, is followed by recovery. The padded floor protects the keel of the bird.

The counter-argument is that the carelessness is attributable to an irresponsible minority, the untrained anglers. The president of the National Federation of Anglers has pointed out 'Most tackle-related incidents involving swans happen on public fisheries between July and September indicating that casual and novice anglers are the main cause of the problem.' A solution is encouraging youngsters to join angling clubs, where they can be taught the Anglers' Code of Conduct. Many hooks and lines can be removed on the riverbank; others may require x-ray diagnosis and surgery under anaesthetic. Costs of operations are borne by rescue groups. Swan rescue groups claim that about 30 per cent of swans in trouble are the victims of fishing tackle injuries but the Swan Sanctuary in Britain, the biggest in Europe, has seen a dramatic decline in such injuries since the 1980s.

Much of this is due to the decrease in lead poisoning. Following the death of mute swans on the Avon at Stratford, in 1979 the Minister of State for the Environment asked the Nature Conservancy Council to investigate. A working group including conservationists and anglers duly did its research and in 1981 concluded that anglers' lead weights were the main cause and should be withdrawn within five years. During that period weights based on other, non-toxic materials could be developed and anglers could phase out the use of lead. Independent research confirmed that almost all swans dying from lead poisoning, some 3,400–4,200 a year, had swallowed anglers' split shot or lead weights. The problem was particularly acute in the coarse fishing areas of Lowland Britain. As a result the mute swan population had fallen when it should have increased with the creation of new habitats such as reservoirs and gravel pits. From 1 January 1987 it became illegal to sell or import a range of anglers' lead weights from 0.06 grams to 28.35 grams. Water authorities were asked to introduce by-laws banning the same range of lead weights from waters under their control. Alternatives developed used materials such as steel and tungsten. Deaths from lead poisoning have been much reduced but not eliminated. During dry spells when water levels are low long necks can reach residual lead in silt. Risking prosecution, some anglers still use illegal sizes, sizes outside the regulations, or a combination of tiny pieces.

Swans also picked up lead shot residual from ducks that had been shot over water and in winter their feeding areas could include fields where grain had been harvested. They ingested the pellets thinking they were grit, needed to help the grinding of food in their gizzards for digestion. Lead is a heavy soft metal easily ground down and able to enter the bloodstream, where it is a cumulative poison. Only three or four pellets are enough to cause poisoning. If corn, a hard grain, is part of their diet then the lead is ground down more quickly, producing a higher concentration in the blood stream. Its principal effect is to paralyse the sphincter muscle in the oesophagus, causing 'kinky neck' and preventing food from passing into the stomach. Result: starvation and death within as little as three weeks. A weakened bird roosting at night may simply stay there and die. Moreover, the problem can be passed on to the next generation. Cygnets are born with inherited high lead levels and do not reach maturity. Non-toxic shot has been required for waterfowl hunting in the United States since 1991 and in Canada since 1999.

Hunters have pursued swans for sport, food and profit. Boats, horses, dogs, guns and nets have all been used to harry, trap and kill the birds, often in large numbers. The largest size of buckshot was swan shot. Fearing invasion of his island, Robinson Crusoe armed himself as best he could: 'the fowling-piece I loaded with near a handful of swan-shot, of the largest size'.[2] This would probably have been at least 0.2 inches (5 mm)

For a swan to be treated it must first be caught.

in diameter. In the United States and Canada during the nineteenth century the trumpeter swan, once fairly common, was hunted almost to extinction. By 1900 it was widely believed that the species had become extinct. Indians and white settlers were both responsible. Fortunately, a small non-migratory trumpeter population survived in remote mountain valleys of Montana, Idaho and Wyoming, where in 1919 two nests were found in Yellowstone National Park. More survived in remote parts of Canada and Alaska. Tundra swans were hunted to a lesser extent, partly because they stayed over open water. A unique way of collecting them in winter was by stealth. In boats covered by pieces of ice hunters dressed in white would paddle or float at night into a flock, where they would knock birds on the head and neck with a pole.

Hunting has not ceased in the United States. It continues in certain states under permit and illegal shooting still takes place, sometimes under the pretext of mistaken identity. Inexperienced hunters say they can confuse tundra swans with snow geese.

Why were the birds hunted? Wherever they appeared they were regarded as fair game, a big bag for sportsmen, especially during the eighteenth and nineteenth centuries. There was more prestige in shooting a swan than the general run of game. The trumpeter swan was a big bird that could be exploited. Swan skins were used in the fur trade, to make boas and ladies' powder puffs. To satisfy demand, from the 1770s the Hudson's Bay Company was a major exporter from Canada, for example shipping 17,671 skins between 1853 and 1877. Most of these would have been from trumpeter swans. Phineas Fogg, who was to travel *Around the World in Eighty Days* (1864), dined at the Reform Club, where 'he was served by the gravest waiters, in dress coats, and shoes with swan-skin soles'.[3] Swan's feet, softened by rubbing with grease, were turned into purses, wallets and tobacco pouches.

Flight feathers were used for adornment of hats, fans and muffs, fashionable worldwide. In London in 1906, for instance, 37,000 ounces (over 1 tonne) of feathers of all kinds were sold at auction. New York and Paris were also sales centres.[4] The business has not entirely ceased. Traditional ceremonial headdress lingers on, for example in the helmets of generals and for Gentlemen at Arms, the Queen's bodyguard. For these the London-based Plumery hand sews small flexible scapular feathers end to end to form a 'fall'. Up to 60 falls are laid together and bound at one end to produce ornamental plumes. Soft down feathers stuffed pillows and mattresses, in France a *duvet de cygne*. Feather beds were a sign of wealth. Hosts of Queen Elizabeth I, who was famous for sleeping around the country, doubtless went out of their way to ensure her bedding and upholstery were of the standard she was used to in London, where Thames swans were plucked annually for her continued comfort.[5] For reassurance of quality, plumes adorned four-

poster beds. Swansdown trimmed dresses and dressing gowns, quilted versions of which used it as stuffing. Madame Bovary was particularly fond of her lover's gift:

> There were even 'my slippers' – a pair to which she had taken a fancy and which Léon had given her. They were of pink satin and trimmed with swansdown. When she sat on his knees, her legs would dangle in the air, while the pretty heelless slippers swung on the toes of her bare feet.[6]

'The last of the Victorian courtesans', dubbed 'Skittles', Catherine Walters (1839–1920), was known too as 'the girl with the swansdown seat'.[7] Delicate and pure, the product also had applications in surgery.

Swan quills made pens more expensive than the more common goose quill, but they were a more pliable and responsive tool, especially on a material with a rough surface like parchment or vellum – the terms are interchangeable – which supplanted papyrus about 190 BCE. They were a pen particularly suited to forming the thick and thin strokes of Roman formal capital letters and also enabled scribes to produce a fine flourish. Quills, with the advantage of featherweight, were first used around the sixth and seventh centuries. They were principally made from large flight feathers, which had the longest barrels and were in their best condition at the time of moulting. They were sorted according to length and size of the barrels and graded into primes, seconds and pinions. Swan quills, being the largest, were more durable than those of the goose, a single swan pen outlasting as many as 50 made from goose quills. Pens were normally sold in bundles, typical quantities being 25 or as many as 100. Quality was estimated by size and weight of the barrels, the term for the weight being a German unit, the loth, equivalent to about 155 grams ($5^1/_2$ oz). Nine-loth or more quills were considered suitable for pens, those of swans ranging from 12 to 26. Queen Victoria favoured one of 25 loths.

The best swan feathers, it was claimed, came from countries with the coldest climate, being exported in bundles of a 'long thousand' (1,200). Sources in the eighteenth and nineteenth centuries included Canada, Germany, Greenland, Iceland, Ireland, Norway, Poland and Russia. The latter were much in demand because of their large dimensions, some having a barrel of more than 20 centimetres (8 inches). Feathers were cut down to the average size of modern ballpoint pens, the cellulose extracted and the barrel, which has a greasy external surface, hardened by heat. Various methods were employed, including heating in the hot ashes of a fire or a bath of hot sand, silver or white. Today a microwave can be used. Finally the quill had to be trimmed to requirements with a quill knife, a skilled operation that had to be repeated during the life of the quill, hence the term penknife. The shafts of quills that curve to the right when held in the hand for writing are taken from the left wing, which curves into the body of the bird, and vice versa. Most mediaeval portraits of scribes show them using short quills and not the large dramatic Hollywood imaginations. Full-feather pens are not so easy to use and could get into the eyes of a scribe bent over his desk.

A scribe who had an impact on writing was the monk Alcuin of York (735–804). At that time the library at York probably had the best collection of books north of the Alps. An adviser to the illiterate Holy Roman Emperor Charlemagne (742–814), Alcuin rationalized the various scripts across the Empire into the Carolingian or Caroline script, on which all Western alphabets and type have since been based. From his work came the foundation of many monastic schools and their work in transcribing and preserving classical manuscripts. They made the Dark Ages, a period of barbarism after the civilization of Rome, less dark. For over a thousand years, the span of the Middle Ages, until the fifteenth-century invention of printing with movable type, quills were the instrument for reproducing the written word. With them copyists transmitted the scriptures, liturgy, history, literature, law, philosophy and science, ensuring their survival and distribution, however limited. Surviving mediaeval manuscripts have become treasures in their own right.

Quills continued to be used for ceremonial and special occasions such as signing acts of parliament, constitutions, legal documents, treaties and the like. They remained in general use until the early 1820s, when the pressed steel nib began to be mass manufactured. Nevertheless institutions such as the Bank of England continued to use traditional writing instruments, purchasing its last batch of quills in 1900. To this day Lloyd's of London use primary feathers to record shipping accidents in the Casualty Book standing in the centre of the underwriting room. The practice harks back to the eighteenth-century origin of Lloyd's as a coffee house where the underwriters in their boxes wrote their business with quills. Individual calligraphers such as Donald Jackson, who achieved his ambition in becoming a scribe to the Crown Office at the House of Lords, i.e., 'The Queen's Scribe', take pleasure in keeping the craft alive. Part of it is illumination, the art of decorating an initial letter, word or text with designs and colours, among them metallic gold. Laying down real gold leaf is a delicate process because the slightest moisture, even a breath of air, will mean that as it is being applied the sheet of leaf sticks to the handler not the manuscript. Hence a feather was often used as a tool, a method carried over by some bookbinders. Today modern gold blocking is done with metal foils.

Another delicate operation is gently removing bees from a honeycomb. Feathers were a useful tool because they did little damage to the bees and the bees could not get caught up in them. Brushes, even though specially made, have the disadvantage of gathering bees in the bristles. A free alternative is a tuft of longish grass. Feathers are also used in marbling, the technique of staining or colouring to make an object look like variegated marble. The flowing, curved patterns are controlled by dragging the surface of the fluid colours with, among other tools, feathers. Swan feathers have the advantage of being light and long, making it easier to reproduce the imprecise meandering qualities of a fine interconnecting vein. Moistened in solvent, the feather picks up the glaze on the fronds and sweeps it across the surface of the ground. The tip of the feather is an excellent tool for applying very thin layers of paint and creating fine detail. When the technique was popular in Europe in the seventeenth and eighteenth centuries and in the United States in the nineteenth for endpapers on books and book edges, marblers were secretive about their craft. Marbling, for various decorative purposes, is now largely a craft activity.

Sign-writing brushes were named after birds such as the swan, eagle and condor, depending upon the number of fibres it was possible to fit inside a quill formed from one of their feathers. These fulfilled the function now performed by the metal 'ferrule' having the handle at one end and the hair in the other. Several quills bound together with wire formed French polishers' mops. By the beginning of the twenty-first century, when signs were being generated on computers, demand for sign-writers' brushes had almost ceased.

Ian Davie, a contemporary British artist who has developed a technique for painting on individual swan feathers, which he regards as a natural canvas. Secondary wing feathers, typically

One of the uses of feathers is artistic. Ian Davie's *Pied Flycatcher amongst Hawthorn Blossom* and *Whilst the Farmer's Away the Sparrows will play - House Sparrows* are painted on swan feathers – birds of a feather.

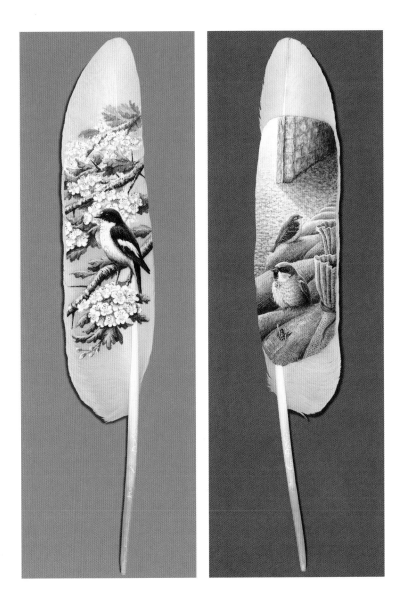

30–43 centimetres (12–17 inches) long, have to be specially treated to create a surface that will accept a delicate primer and acrylic paint. These are applied with tiny brushes that will not damage the feather. Not all of the surface is painted on, only the centre section, leaving untouched feather top and bottom, a work of art in itself. The subjects Ian Davie chooses for his delicate miniatures are from wild life: birds, animals, fishes and the like. Not to spoil the subject, he signs them on the side of the quill. The finished artwork is mounted and framed.

Although new materials, techniques and changes of attitude have made wide use of swan feathers unnecessary or unacceptable, all the surviving applications have made demand exceed supply. Swans were still being hunted commercially in the Soviet Union into the 1940s and, in New Zealand, under the Wildlife Act 1953, black swans can be hunted under specific conditions and at the discretion of the minister responsible for the Department of Conservation. Growth of the conservation movement in the latter half of the twentieth century has limited the sources of feathers.

Among tribal peoples, who hunted with bows and arrows, plumage had a practical and ritual application. Swan feathers were used in fly-tying, especially for catching salmon. Sewn together, swan breasts made bed coverings and clothes for special occasions, possibly including re-enactment of legends such as those of swan-maidens. It is not difficult to imagine young women waving wings in symbolic dances. To preserve the pure white of the plumage such clothes would have been brought out only for significant events or days in the calendar. At Hiawatha's wedding feast in Longfellow's poem,

> He was dressed in shirt of doeskin . . .
> On his head were plumes of swan's down.[8]

Bird bones had a variety of uses. Making imprints with joints of leg bones was a quick and simple way of decorating unfired pottery. Bones made beads, drinking tubes, musical instruments and whistles, some of which would have been used in rituals. In the Yukon, for example, in puberty rites girls drank water through swans' wing bones to ensure lightness of step and easy pregnancies.

Many shamans, healers who were in mystical communion with the spirit world, regarded swans as having spiritual power. Receiving his power from the creature that selected him, he acted accordingly. Thus among the Nganasan people of Siberia a shaman imitated the flight of the swan and uttered its sounds. In North America some shamans had swans as their 'doctors' and swansdown was a healing material, often to be found in an Indian medicine bag. Ceremonial swansdown was contained in the feet, necks and heads of swans. Specially prepared swansdown was placed in amulets given to sufferers from minor ailments. When a baby was born its umbilical cord was mixed with some swansdown and put into a round beaded case sewn by the mother. Sinews twisted with swansdown worn on each finger and as armbands and garters ensured that her hands and limbs were flexible and strong for work. North American tribes wore swan masks in dances during the last feast of winter, when the shaman's spirit helped bring back swans and other migrating birds for spring. Swans heralded the arrival of spring, a season of new life to be celebrated after the hardships of winter, and the swan mask represented the spirit of the bird. The mask was often surrounded by swan feathers and appendages, made of wood and feathers, which the shaman rattled loudly as he imitated cries of the bird. Even today there is a spring Celebration of Swans at Whitehorse, capital of the Yukon, and at Marsh Lake, their main staging post in the area.

Among man-made hazards for swans are overhead power cables, which they can fly into. Swans have slow flight, low manoeuvrability and poor forward vision, especially in mists, making them susceptible to this type of accident. A bird may be electrocuted, stunned or damaged by the collision, which can also cut off electricity supply to an area. Swans are big birds so when they land after hitting a wire they come down very heavily, perhaps sustaining a bad injury such as a broken leg or wing. They can become 'one wingers'. Burns and wounds have to be treated. Whatever the injury it causes stress in the bird. Stunned, it may take time to recover, during which time it is at the mercy of predators, such as foxes and crows, which may peck out the eyes. Having consulted bird protection groups, some electricity companies are trying to reduce the scale of the problem by installing diverters, brightly coloured plastic discs about the size of a tea plate, on lengths of power lines where the risks are greatest. Typical areas, often scenic, are where lines cross wetlands and during migration the large birds fly low. Fitting diverters is an inexpensive procedure that can be carried out on relatively short stretches of line during routine maintenance. Putting cables underground is more costly.

Part of the wirescape is telecommunications towers, necessary for the growing use of mobile phones. Standalone units like chimney stacks, they present less of a hazard than wind turbines massed in farms, which are accounting for a greater proportion of deaths from collisions. These are most likely to occur when birds are climbing to an altitude in limited visibility during the first two hours of night during migration. Young birds are most at risk. They can fly into the moving arms of a turbine ('mincing machines') or the surrounding network of power lines. With governments putting greater emphasis on generating more electricity from clean sustainable sources, the problem is set to grow, to the dismay of ornithological and environmental organizations. One solution is not to develop wind farms in the path of migration and flight patterns, especially where birds are flying low at the end of a long flight, as for instance whooper swans do having migrated from Iceland to the Western Isles of Scotland. Illumination of turbines is not recommended. In conditions of poor visibility, light may even attract birds, increasing the risk of collision.

Minor hazards include windows and vehicle windscreens. Young birds have been known to mistake aircraft runways and wet roads for a stretch of water. In places where there are likely hazards, such as where swans venture across roads near rivers, Highways staff are often trained to capture them safely and without causing distress. One example is where the M25 (the busy ring road around London) crosses the River Thames.

An unlikely transgressor of the law, taking advantage of a collision, was the Master of the Queen's Music, Sir Peter Maxwell Davies. In the spring of 2005 near his home on the island of Sanday in the Orkneys, off the north-east coast of Scotland, he found the carcase of a migrating whooper swan that had flown into power lines and died. He informed the Royal Society for the Protection of Birds, which advised him to dispose of the bird. Instead he left it maturing outside his cottage ready for making some fresh swan terrine from the best parts, the breast and leg meat, rather than feeding them to his cat. The dark, rich meat tasted 'a bit like pheasant with a hint of venison'. His culinary intention was interrupted by a visit from the police with a search warrant under the Wildlife and Countryside Act 1981. They seized the carcase as evidence and cautioned the 70-year-old Queen's composer that anything he said could be used in evidence. Naturally he informed Buckingham Palace. The police also took away a pair of swan's wings they found in the shed. Sir Peter was keeping them to give the Sunday school as a replacement for the dusty ones the Angel Gabriel wore in its nativity play. Not wanting to be corrupted, the two polite but firm police officers refused his offer of some terrine he had made from an earlier swan victim. He also voluntarily handed over a swan leg from the freezer.

To the press he joked that he might be locked up in the Tower of London, a term of imprisonment that 'would inspire some very interesting music'. His first important work as the Queen's composer, *Reconciliation '45*, a composition to mark the sixtieth anniversary of the end of the Second World War, was due to be performed in London in midsummer. Of course Sir Peter was in no way responsible for the death of the whooper swan, a protected species. Had it been a mute swan, the case would have been different. In 1910 the Queen's ownership of all mute swans was contested in Orkney. A local lawyer shot one to prove that the ancient 'udal' Viking law, which stated that islanders have absolute ownership of their land, still had force there. He won his case.[9]

6 Food

Being large birds, swans have been an obvious source of food since prehistoric times, the end of the Ice Age. Bones have been found, for instance, in Mesolithic and Neolithic sites on the foreshores of the Shannon Estuary in the west of Ireland. The birds may have been clubbed or grabbed in nests while flightless during the breeding season, trapped in nooses or snares, or shot with arrows having blunt wooden heads. *Kyudo*, the traditional art of Japanese archery, began in prehistory among hunter-gatherers, who used swan feathers on their arrows. They are still used in modern times, now *kyudo* is a martial art practised as a form of physical, moral and spiritual development. In the first century AD, at the Early Iron Age lake village of Glastonbury, Somerset, slings and clay pellets were used for catching waterfowl. Archaeological evidence includes some unfired pellets, swan remains and dome-shaped clay ovens.

In the Old Testament the swan, a dark meat, was classified as unclean. According to Leviticus, 'These are they which ye shall have in abomination among the fowls; they shall not be eaten, they are an abomination . . . the swan, and the pelican and the gier eagle.'[1] The command was repeated in Deuteronomy.[2] There was some justification for the prohibition since swan meat is tough and hard to digest. Cygnets are tastier, especially if fattened with oats, which reduce the fishy taste. However, the birds were raised for the table, being eaten in Europe from the eighth to the eighteenth centuries. A swanherd, an occupation still surviving at Abbotsbury at the west end of Chesil Beach in Dorset, was a person who tended swans. Benedictine monks established Abbotsbury swannery to encourage the birds to continue nesting in their natural habitat so that cygnets could be raised in pens for serving at feasts. The hunt-loving stylish pilgrim monk described by Chaucer (1340–1400) in the *Canterbury Tales* 'liked a fat swan best, and roasted whole'. For those who could afford it, a religious occasion such as a saint's feast day or, say, the period from Christmas to Twelfth Night was sufficient reason to indulge. Following Henry VIII's dissolution of the monasteries in 1536–40, the Strangways family bought the Abbotsbury swannery in 1543, signifying their ownership of the birds by a small nick in the web of the foot. After 1756, when a member of the family became Earl of Ilchester, this was named the Hive of Ilchester swan-mark. In 1992 the Post Office issued a set of commemorative stamps to mark the sexcentenary of Abbotsbury, then thought to have been founded in 1392. Ten years later an earlier written record was discovered, putting the date back by almost 40 years to 1354. Today over a thousand mute swans live on the lagoon, a tourist attraction.

From the Middle Ages swans were kept on rivers and fattened in ponds as Robert May's *The Accomplisht Cook* (1678) advises:

Fatting of Swans and Cygnets

For Swans and their feeding, where they build their nests, you shall suffer them to remain undisturbed, and it will be sufficient because they can better order themselves in that business than any man.

Feed your Cygnets in all sorts as you feed your Geese, and they will be through fat in seven or eight weeks. If

The swan pit at the Great Hospital, Norwich, in the early 20th century. Cygnets had been fattened there since the Middle Ages.

you will have them sooner fat, you shall feed them in some pond hedged, or placed in for that purpose.[3]

Malt, barley and maize were the preferred fattening foods, and the young birds were at their best in October and November. After their first Christmas they deteriorated. In *The English Hus-Wife* (1615) Gervais Markham recommended that large fowls with black flesh such as swan should be 'brown roasted' a long time before a slow fire. William Rabisha (*fl.* 1625–1661), cook and author, included a recipe for baked swan in *The Whole Body of Cookery Dissected, Taught, and Fully Manifested* (1661) 'for the instruction of young practitioners' preparing for large aristo-cratic occasions. Such birds were not only for consumption by their well-to-do owners but also gifts for important people. Ownership was restricted to freeholders, set in 1483 at property greater than five marks. Examination of the tariffs 1274–1638 of the Company of Poulters has shown that the swan was the most expensive bird. In 1274 its set price was three shillings, against twopence halfpenny for a best capon, fivepence for a goose and

fourpence for a pheasant. Hence it was also the most profitable to raise. The Brewers' Company was famous for the excellence of the swans served up at its banquets. It was a bird fit for a king such as Henry VIII at his Hampton Court feasts. *A Noble Book of Royal Feasts* printed by Richard Pynson in London in 1500 contained a recipe for roasted swan.

Like other large birds such as cranes, herons and peacocks, they were usually roasted. A fifteenth-century manuscript outlines the process:

> Cut a swan in the roof of the mouth toward the brain end-long, and let him bleed, and keep the blood for entrails; or else knit a knot in his neck. And so let his neck break; then scald him. Draw him and roast him even as thou do goose in all points, and serve him forth with entrails.[4]

The bird was accompanied by a black sauce called chawdron, the recipe for which does not sound very appetising:

Take gizzards, and livers, and heart of Swan; and if the guts are fatty, slit them, clean them, and cast them thereto, and boil them in fair water: and then take them up, and hew them small, and then cast them into the same broth, (but strain it through a strainer first); and cast thereto powdered pepper, cinnamon, and vinegar, and salt, and let boil. And then take the blood of the Swan, and fresh broth, and bread, and draw them though a strainer, and cast thereto; and let boil together. And then take powder of ginger, when it is almost enough, & put thereto, and serve forth with the swan.[5]

Sometimes the neck was cut off, stuffed and served separately as 'pudding de swan neck'. Potted swan became fashionable in the mid-seventeenth century. The flesh was beaten hard, mixed with fat bacon until it was like dough, then seasoned with salt, pepper and other spices before it was baked in a pot for eight to ten hours in claret and butter. It was butter-sealed in a pot. Swan could also be mixed with other game such as boar and venison for raised pies, also butter-sealed. According to Gervais Markham, the best crust was made from rye paste.

At court feasts cooked animals were displayed in a lifelike pose, as though they had not been cooked. Thus a swan was carefully skinned before being cooked so that the feathers remained on the skin. It was then drawn, stuffed with highly seasoned forcemeat or small birds, which had themselves been plucked. The bird was held in a natural pose by skewers. Its head was either cut off and put aside or sprinkled with cold water during roasting. Just before being served, it was re-dressed in its skin with feathers arrayed, its feet and beak gilded with powdered gold. Less well-off hosts could make do with a flour paste coloured with saffron. Wired wings simulated flight. As the bird was brought in on a silver dish to musical accompaniment a piece of lighted camphor in its beak issued sparks to add to the spectacle. A bizarre alternative of cotton soaked in *aqua ardens* ('burning water', meaning distilled alcohol) was employed by Chiquart, the chief cook at the Savoy court in the early part of the fifteenth century. When ignited, the bird appeared to be breathing fire.[6] The meat of valiant knights, it was presented to the guest of honour, by squires on routine occasions, by a company of ladies on great occasions. Before carving the bird the hero of the event made a vow, not necessarily one to be fulfilled.

It was the arrival of the turkey from the New World in the sixteenth century that began to lessen the appeal of the swan as the bird for a banquet or the Christmas dinner. It was easier to raise and more pleasant to eat. Feasts at which swans were served did not die out with the Middle Ages, though. The wedding feast of

George Flegel's
Large Food Display
(c. 1630).

Tsar Alexei in 1670 consisted of roast swan with saffron.[7] In his
long 1717 poem *Alma* the diplomat Matthew Prior noted 'If you
dine with my Lord May'r, Roast-Beef and Ven'son is your Fare;
Thence You proceed to Swan and Bustard.'[8]

In the eighteenth century, to increase income at the Great
Hospital, Norwich, the swan pit for raising cygnets was rebuilt.
The pit, linked to the River Wensum with sluice gates to maintain water levels, was restored in the late nineteenth century,
altered in the twentieth and since 2002 is a Grade II listed building. Raising cygnets for feasts was a privilege the master of the
hospital had enjoyed since the Middle Ages. As late as the 1880s
80–100 cygnets were being fattened each year. Their wings were

The swan has
pride of place in
this oil painting
of 1644 by
David Teniers
the younger
(1610–1690).

145

Swans served whole at a feast in Sergei Eisenstein's film *Ivan the Terrible* (1944).

clipped and their bills cut with a distinctive pattern bearing the hospital's own mark. Fattened swans were taken from the swan pit with the aid of a long pole having an iron end similar to a shepherd's crook, killed, plucked by hand, a laborious but sociable task, and then sold to bodies such as Oxford and Cambridge colleges. The Feast book of St John's College, Cambridge, records that swans were being eaten at Christmas 1879–94 in dishes such as swans' giblet soup. The leading Catholic in England, the Duke of Norfolk, sent one to the Pope. The Hospital sent out plucked, trussed swans ready for the oven with printed cooking instructions:

> Take three pounds of beef, beat fine in a mortar.
> Put into the Swan – that is, when you've caught her.
> Some pepper, salt mace, some nutmeg, an onion
> Will heighten the flavour in Gourmand's opinion.
> Then tie it up tight with a small piece of tape,

That the gravy and other things may not escape.
A meal paste (rather stiff) should be laid on the breast,
And some whited brown paper should cover the rest.
Fifteen minutes at least ere the swan you take down,
Pull the paste off the bird, that the breast may get brown.
To a gravy of beef (good and strong) I opine
You'll be right if you add half a pint of port wine:
Pour this through the swan – yes, quite through the belly,
Then serve the whole up with some hot currant jelly.

                      N.B. The swan must not be skinned.[9]

In the Australian section of *Mrs Beeton's All About Cookery*
(1923) there is a recipe for Black Swan, Roasted or Baked:

This bird should be quite young, otherwise it is better
cooked in hashes or stews. Very frequently it is cooked in
the same way as a goose, but is very nice stuffed with
farce made from minced beefsteak in the same manner as
sausage farce, substituting beef for the pork. Truss as for
goose, squeeze lemon-juice over and wrap in bacon rashers.

A moulded
savoury at a
Vintners' Company
feast in London.

Bake for about 2 hours in a moderate oven, remove the
rashers an hour before serving, and baste well and dredge
flour over till crisp and brown.

TIME – About 2 hours. SUFFICIENT for 8 persons.[10]

In the mid-nineteenth century the chef Francatelli recommended a roasting time of four hours.

The bird could be served in various ways. When the young
politician Disraeli met the new Member of Parliament
William Gladstone at the Lord Chancellor's dinner on 17
January 1835 he reported to his sister 'we had a swan very
white and tender, and stuffed with truffles, the best company
there'.[11] During food rationing in the Second World War, the
restaurateur Joe Bertorelli (1893–1994) 'used swan in pies and
corned beef in bolognese' at The Monte Carlo in Queensway,
West London. 'The staff ate horsemeat.'[12]

Swan eggs could also be eaten. In New Zealand they were an
ingredient of a malt chocolate drink, a practice stopped under
pressure from poultry farmers. Alternative uses were in
Christmas baking or, more likely, in the feeding of racehorses.

A copperplate extract from the Great Hospital account book.

Ice cream is more appealing when moulded.

7 Conservation

In 966 the English King Edgar gave rights to the abbots of Croyland in Lincolnshire over local straying mute swans, which suggests that by that date somebody else owned swans that could be distinguished by a mark of some kind. Under the feudal system the Crown granted ownership rights to lords of the manor and dignitaries such as abbots and bishops throughout the kingdom. Henry de Bracton's systematic treatment of English law *De Legibus et Consuetudinibus Angliae* (1235–59) included a section on the ownership of animals and swans. Certainly the birds had royal protection from at least the Late Middle Ages. Under a 1483 Act of Edward IV:

> None (but the King's Son) shall have any Mark or Game of *Swans* of his own, or to his use, except he have Lands and Tenements of Freehold worth five marks per Annum [approximately £900 today], besides Reprises; in pain to have them seised by any having lands of that value, to be divided betwixt the King and Seizor.

A swan-mark, a distinctive pattern of notches cut in the upper mandible of the bill, identified the owner, was registered and a gift of inheritance that could be handed down to one's heirs. Marks could be based on armorial bearings, initials, tools of a trade or profession, an association with a patron saint. Designs were

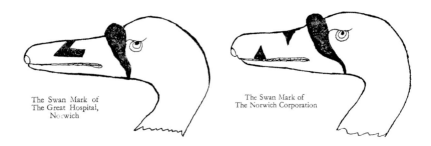

The Swan Mark of
The Great Hospital,
Norwich

The Swan Mark of
The Norwich Corporation

recorded in swan-rolls and disputes could be settled in courts of swan-mote. All unmarked swans were the property of the Crown.

Tudor monarchs were particularly protective. Eggs were protected under a 1496 Act of Henry VII: 'None shall take out of the nest any eggs of Falcon, Goshawk, Lanner or Swan, in pain of a Year and a day's imprisonment, and to incur a fine at the King's pleasure, to be divided between the King and the Owner of the Ground.' Henry VIII decreed that no one who owned swans could appoint a new swanherd without a licence from the royal swanherd. A 1564 proclamation of Queen Elizabeth on the conservation of swans stated 'It is ordeyned, that no man shal take no gray swannes nor white swannes flying.' In 1570 the *Order of Swannes* laid down that those who erased or counterfeited any owner's marks should be imprisoned for a year. Swan ownership was probably at its highest in Elizabethan times (1558–1603). Under the first Stuart king, James I (reigned 1603–25), the penalty for stealing eggs was reduced from a year's imprisonment to three months or a payment of 20 shillings for each egg to the churchwardens for the use of the poor. Penalties for killing a swan continued to be severe. A mid-nineteenth-century poster gives transportation to the penal colony of Australia as a sentence actually enacted. The Vintners' Company records show a sentence of seven weeks with hard labour as late as 1895.

Beak markings made by the nicks of a knife distinguished ownership of the birds.

Today the Crown's right over swans is part of the *Wild Creatures & Forest Laws Act* (1971). The Act sought to abolish some of the more esoteric feudal laws still on the statute book but the Queen refused to allow the Royal Prerogative to be interfered with. Speaking on the bill in the House of Lords, the Lord Chancellor noted, 'In order to be the object of the Royal Prerogative the swan must be white, swimming in open and common rivers, wild and unmarked. Why the black swan should be discriminated against in this way I do not know. Perhaps the Race Relations Board will tell me.'

From the twelfth century, marking of swans was done at the annual ceremony of swan-upping, i.e. taking out of the water, which amounted to an annual census of the swan population on stretches of the River Thames. In the seventeenth century the term became corrupted to swan-hopping, probably because of an intrusive misplaced 'h' in Cockney dialect. In the ceremony owners went out with a representative of the royal swanherd and possible pageantry to round up the well-grown cygnets. Records of this census were kept, for instance by the Oxford college Christ Church. The colourful ceremony, with officials dressed in scarlet uniforms, is still performed towards the end of July on the Thames. Formerly it covered the stretch from London Bridge to Henley in Oxfordshire, where swans were also picked up before the Henley regatta. As swans no longer breed on the tideway the length has been reduced to the shorter Sunbury–Abingdon stretch, a five-day exercise. On passing Windsor Castle, the rowers stand to attention in their boat with oars raised and salute 'Her Majesty The Queen, Seigneur of the Swans'.[1]

There are now only two non-royal owners on the river, both City livery companies, the Dyers' and Vintners', whose rights were granted in the late fifteenth century when they had halls by the river. In the company of the Queen's Swan Marker, the swan

wardens of the two companies and their uniformed assistants look for broods of cygnets. When one is sighted a cry of 'All up!' is given and the rowing skiffs get into position. The birds are landed, checked and fitted with an engraved and numbered leg ring. Until 1996 their bills were nicked with a sharp knife, cygnets having the same mark as their parents, the Dyers making one notch on the bill, the Vintners two. Royal birds remain unmarked, a practice followed since the reign of Edward VII (1901–10), when Queen Alexandra was concerned that the birds were being hurt by the complex marks used since the reign of George III (1760–1820). At the end of each year's ceremony the Dyers' Company has a banquet, the main item on the menu being 'Dyers' cygnet', in modern times roast goose.[2]

Apart from officiating at swan-upping, the Queen's Swan Marker has other duties. He advises organizations throughout the country on swan welfare, monitors the health of local swan populations, and briefs fishing and boating groups on how to work with existing wildlife and maintaining natural habitats. Much of his work involves swan rescue organizations, of which there are a large number. Another annual duty is co-ordinating the temporary removal of swans from the areas along stretches of the Thames where summer rowing regattas are held.

Elsewhere conservation is a comparatively recent concept, at its strongest since the latter part of the twentieth century. For example, the Kronotsky Nature Reserve, established in 1934 on the east coast of the Kamchatka Peninsula in eastern Russia, had its boundaries extended in 1967. In 1969 the Baikalsky Nature Reserve by Lake Baikal in south-eastern Russia was designated for research into natural sciences. In the United States and Canada in the nineteenth and early twentieth centuries the trumpeter swan was hunted almost to extinction. Although the Canada/United States Migratory Bird Treaty was signed in 1916 the regulations were weak and were particularly ineffective in the Yukon and Alaska. Survival figures vary but are all of the same order. According to one census, in 1933 there were 73 trumpeter swans breeding in Canada and 50 in the United States. Gradually moves were made to restore the balance of nature. Red Rock Lakes National Wildlife Refuge, Montana, opened in 1935, gave the swans food and shelter in the coldest weather and a safe area in which to breed. Nobody could kill them for meat or feathers. The Trumpeter Swan Society, formed in 1968, acted as a voice for the birds. By 1984 there was a North American management Plan for Trumpeter Swans. Under restoration programmes, they have been reintroduced to their old nesting sites. Eggs were collected, incubated and the young adults held in captivity for two years, the most difficult survival period, before release. Experiments with foster parents of other species, cross-fostering, were carried out, with less success. For identification released birds were fitted with a US Fish and Wildlife Service leg band. Survival comparisons were made with the release of cygnets imprinted on a swan decoy, which they regarded as their parent. These birds, living under supervision in remote marshes until they could fly, learned to avoid potential predators through responses to taped sounds associated with the decoy.

Reintroduction can only be sustainable though if the first generation is taught migration routes. In Canada the Migratory Bird Research Group embarked in 1996 on an ambitious venture using light aircraft mounted on amphibious floats for a short take-off. Acting both as a leader encouraging birds to follow and as a sheep dog to keep them in formation, the plane first exercises the young swans and then shows them their migration route. Success was achieved in 1998 when a new flock of trumpeter swans was migrated from Sudbury, Ontario, to Muscatatuck National Wildlife Refuge in southern Indiana. In subsequent springs some were sighted back in Sudbury.[3] There is a problem of too many trumpeters landing in the same place, where they can exhaust the food supply and are at risk of disease. Moving them on first necessitates capture. One way of capturing them is to stun them temporarily by shining a spotlight on them. They can then be bundled up and transported for release.

Although the total population is still small compared to what it once was, the future of the largest waterfowl in North America has been assured. The tundra swan has fared better, its numbers growing to the point where some states have allowed hunting to stabilize the population, which might otherwise cause excessive property damage.

The leading advocate of conservation in the United States was Richard Pough (1904–2003), author of the National Audubon Society guides to the birds of North America. His concern was sparked in 1939 when his wife came home wearing a new hat decorated with feathers. They were coming back into fashion through a loophole in the law that allowed the importation of wild bird feathers for fly-fishing. The following year Pough launched a campaign against the practice in an article *Massacre for Millinery*, which won the support of the film star Mary Pickford and Eleanor Roosevelt, wife of the president. The hat

Swans at night in
Reykjavik, Iceland.

industry soon gave in. In 1948 Pough left the Audubon Society to
become chairman of conservation and ecology at the American
Museum of Natural History but his links were not severed. In
1951 his *Audubon Water Bird Guide* was published. The founding
president of Nature Conservancy (1950), he devoted his energies
to preserving wildlife sanctuaries.[4]

The influence of what Peter Scott had started in England in
1946 as a single wetland site spread. In 1971 an international con-
vention on saving wetlands for wildlife and people was signed in
Ramsar, Iran. The 121 signatories were obliged to designate and
protect their significant wetlands and to promote their 'wise use'.
Over a thousand sites are now on the Ramsar list of Wetlands of
International Importance, over 600 of them in Europe. Peter
Scott's single site in the UK, Slimbridge, has expanded to nine

under the Wildfowl and Wetlands Trust, the last one opened in millennium year on the site of four disused Victorian reservoirs in south-west London. On a smaller scale the extraction of gravel and sand for the construction industry leaves pits that can become environmentally attractive lakes beckoning wildlife. Similarly, growth in the number of marinas to accommodate the increasing amount of leisure boats is creating new habitats for wildfowl. Salt water does not present a problem because glands above a swan's eyes extract salt from the bloodstream and excrete it through the nostrils.

The RSPB, founded in 1891 as the Society for the Protection of Birds and made Royal in 1904, campaigned on issues such as the use of lead shot, the siting of airports and wind farms. It also purchased tracts of marshland such as 352 hectares at Rainham on the Greater London/Essex border to preserve them for grazing. Its reserves were not only homes for birds but also education

Diversions at the Marquis of Lafayette's summer residence included feeding the swans, as seen in this lithograph, c. 1882.

centres where children could learn about them and their responsibilities towards them, for example when fishing. Various bodies have established rescue centres and sanctuaries, where birds can be taken by ambulance for treatment. In the UK the National Swan Sanctuary at Shepperton near London has an operating theatre, an x-ray room, an intensive care ward, an isolation ward, a washing room for oiled swans, nursing ponds and rehabilitation lakes. Established in the early 1980s in a small back garden, it now has associate rescue centres around England, in Ireland and The Netherlands. In Germany the city of Hamburg employs a swan keeper. Every autumn with the aid of fellow council workers he rounds up swans on the inner city Lake Alster and takes them by boat to their winter quarters. There they are fed and cared for until the spring.

Concerned individuals and small groups in many countries also devote their time and resources to swan welfare. This may be anything from fund-raising to being on call, gaining access to difficult sites, wading into unknown waters, wrapping victims in a swan jacket, to providing tender nursing care on their own property. Often these volunteers develop a personal interest, giving the birds names and following their progress after treatment. Birds are then normally returned to their natural habitat. Through the work in recent years of swan sanctuaries, particularly involving vets, much more is known about the ills to which the birds are subject and how they can be treated. Food poisoning, botulism, was a common diagnosis, sometimes mistaken for lead poisoning. It occurs almost exclusively in hot, dry weather and affects other species in a specific area. Aspergillosis, a fungal infection of the lungs caused by mouldy feed and evidenced by breathing difficulties and/or a rattling wet cough, is common in waterfowl. Swans are prone to viral infections. Herpes virus in a virulent strain can cause the extinction of a hundred or more birds in a short time. Duck plague, properly known as duck virus enteritis, also affects geese and swans. It occurs especially when wildfowl are together in high density. To prevent spread of these diseases it is important to remove sick birds from their water and treat them with appropriate veterinary medicines.

More serious both for birds and humans is bird flu, which can cause a pandemic. According to microbiologists, migratory birds, no respecters of borders, probably carry the virus. Remedies are mass culling of birds and vaccination of humans, both in their millions. There was a scare in southern China during February 2004 when authorities confirmed that ten black swans in Shenzen Safari Zoo had been killed by the bird flu virus. Although carriers of the virus, aquatic birds were thought to be immune to the illness. Possibly the virus had mutated. The situation was serious enough for governments, mindful of the 1918 pandemic, which killed at least 21 million people, more than the total casualties in the First World War, to follow World Health Organization recommendations and stock enough vaccine and anti-viral drugs to protect a substantial percentage of their populations. Most of the victims of the 1918 pandemic were in Asia, the source of bird flu. The concern, as then, was that the virus could rapidly be carried westward. By October 2005, carried by wild swans and other birds, it had reached south-eastern Europe in the H_5N1 form that can be deadly to humans.

High density of birds in a particular area presents another problem, conflict between species. For example, mute swans were introduced as graceful ornaments to the Chesapeake Bay region, where the native species is the wintering tundra swan. Under conservation programmes in the final decades of the twentieth century the mute population has soared. Flocks of 600–1,000 birds have been recorded. Moreover, the heavier mute swan, weighing as much as 11 kilograms (25 pounds) against the

Conservation in the belle époque: *Afternoon at the Zoo*, 1882, oil on canvas, by the French painter Jean-Richard Goubie (1842–1899)

Swans in a public park in Lyon, *c.* 1890s.

The logo of the Swan Sanctuary, which has rescue sites in England and southern Ireland. At its London head-quarters it has an operating theatre, an x-ray room, an intensive care ward and a rehabilitation lake.

the **Swan** *sanctuary*

The Mute Swan is the International Symbol for World Peace

tundra's 7, is a voracious eater, a year-round resident consuming much more submerged aquatic vegetation such as widgeon grass, wild celery and various pondweeds, which are slower to recover. With its longer neck it can reach deeper into the water, pulling up plants by their roots or dislodging them by paddling vigorously. It bullies the native species, driving them from feeding grounds over a large area and trampling eggs and chicks of other nesting water birds such as black skimmers and terns. The net result is disruption of the ecology of the Chesapeake Bay region. One consequence is reducing crabbing and fishing opportunities, for which the area is noted. Water quality is affected by the large numbers defecating; excessive wildfowl equals pollution. Population control measures, varying by states, include addling eggs and relocating or killing adult birds.

In 1945 the 11,250-hectare Laguna Blanca National Park, close to Zapala in western Neuquen province of Patagonia, was created to control too many black-necked swans building their nests in the area. There is an even larger area in Chaco, northern Paraguay, where under The Nature Conservancy the coscoroba swan is protected. Sanctuaries do not necessarily guarantee protection. For instance, the Cruces River Nature Sanctuary originated in the 1960 Chilean earthquake, which created new wetlands. An officially designated wetland of international importance under the Ramsar convention, it provided a shelter for, among other birds, black-necked and coscoroba swans, attracting thousands of tourists. Changes soon became evident after the opening of a pulp mill on the Cruces River in early 2004. Swans began dying from starvation and disease, attributed to effluents from the mill killing an aquatic plant that was their main food. It was also believed that contaminants in the waste water were causing neurological damage to the birds, which became too weak to fly or sustain flight. Examination of carcasses revealed serious malnourishment, loss of muscle tissue, unusual levels of iron among other chemicals, and the presence of parasites. Local residents formed Acción Por Los Cisnes (Action for the Swans), securing two temporary closures of the mill for environmental violations. The World Widlife Fund, which in 2005 led a mission to the site, where it found only a few survivors from the estimated 5,000 swan population, has urged the Chilean government and mill owners to develop a plan to end pollution from the mill.

During the latter half of the twentieth century the conservation movement gathered such strength that by the beginning of the twenty-first some groups were wondering whether it was entirely a good thing. There were conflicts with some of man's perfectly legal and highly desirable activities. Was conservation becoming a threat to 'civilization'? Swans, for example, could within days strip rivers of weed under which brown trout hid and insect larvae, shrimp and snails flourished. Bare and desolate riverbeds would take time to recover, during which other birds and animals would be deprived of their food. There were other causes such as unsustainable pesticide pollution from farms and removal of water for drinking and irrigation, but anglers tended to regard swans as the main culprits. Protected birds, especially on the chalk streams of southern England, came to be seen as pests. Should their eggs be pricked or doused in paraffin oil to discourage incubation? Surely in 2004 some method of population control was justified.[5] Taking into account the views of affected parties, the extent of the problem had to be quantified and the relative weight of the contributing factors assessed. Then a management plan could be drafted, opened for public consultation and, if necessary, some action taken.

In the state of Maryland there was particular concern about the depredations of the intruding mute swan, which was destructive and was aggressively pushing out the native tundra species. Even the beauty of the bird was disputed, with examples of its cruelty to other creatures, including pecking out the eyes of a kitten and traumatizing its child owner. There were calls for the birds, out of control and upsetting the balance of Chesapeake Bay's ecosystem, to be culled. Why not issue hunting permits that would also be a source of revenue as in some other states? Some members of the public went as far as calling for the whole state to be declared a swan-free zone. Against this, animal rights activists argued that the birds were being made scapegoats for larger environmental problems. There was widespread public debate involving the state's Department of Natural Resources, the us Fish and Wildlife Service, Maryland Ornithological Society, Audubon Society, and many other interest groups and individuals. In fact swans were said to pose an environmental threat in seventeen Eastern states. The Atlantic Flyway Council representing state wildlife departments recommended a cull of mute swans, reducing the 2002 population of 14,000 to 3,000 by 2013. Opponents included the Committee to Abolish Sport Hunting, Friends of Animals, Fund for Animals and Save Our Swans, with its evocative acronym.[6] In the end the hunters lost. In September 2003 the US Fish and Wildlife Service withdrew all permits for state and federal officials to kill mute swans.

These were local and regional problems. On an international scale there is a conflict between bird conservation and air safety. The first known bird strike was in 1908, the first fatality in 1912, when collision with a gull caused the death of the pilot of a Wright Flyer 1. The hazards have become more severe with the increase in the number and size of aircraft flying and the number of birds being conserved. Moreover, modern aircraft speeds have increased. Although birds have remained the same size, their energy impact in collisions has grown with the square of the relative impact speed. It can be enough to damage the airframe, which includes vital sections such as wing fuel tanks, and shatter windshields, injuring crew with flying glass and causing the aircraft to depressurize. More serious is the effect on turbine engines, which are subject to even higher impact energies. These are due to the high rotation speeds of their fans and compressors, especially during the high thrust demands for take-off. Bird ingestion causes engine damage or failure. Most bird strikes occur at lower altitudes during take-off and landing, but swans can fly as high as 3.5 kilometres (12,000 feet) during migration.

Obviously the risks are greater with large birds, 3.6 kilograms (8 pounds) or more, and in skeins, which can be detected by radar. A radar scan converter sensitive enough to detect a swan would show a little unidentified blob; in a big enough skein it would be possible to make out the formation. Even so risks are enhanced during twice-yearly migrations of swans, what the US Air Force refers to as 'waves of biomass'. One ingested adult swan is enough to disable an aero-engine. The worst accident involving swans occurred in the 1960s at Ellicot, to the west of Baltimore, Maryland, where at night a Vickers Viscount encountered a flock of swans at 1.8 kilometres (6,000 feet). One, weighing 6 kilograms (13 pounds), penetrated the tailplane leading edge, causing the tail to detach and hence loss of control. There were seventeen fatalities. As a consequence the airplane certification standard was changed to include the rule that a tail must not fail if it struck a 3.6 kilogram bird at its design cruising speed.

In 2001 the UK Central Science Laboratory estimated that wildlife strikes to aircraft cost the aviation industry worldwide over $1 billion a year. Reported losses are often underestimates because they do not include lost flying hours, fuel or disruption of passenger and freight transportation. It has been forecast that during the first decade of the twenty-first century the risk of an airliner colliding with large flocking birds will rise by more than 2.5 times and be around 6 times higher in 2010 than in 1990.[7] Clearly, management of the large flocking bird hazard involves applying bird control techniques well beyond airport perimeters. Areas within a 16 kilometre (10 mile) radius of an airport could be affected. This will involve changes in attitudes. For example, landowners are only too willing to control animals, particularly vermin, that destroy their animals and crops. Some birds are regarded as pests, many as worthy of protection. Conservationists, who may also on occasions be air passengers, have to take the needs of aviation into account when establishing refuges for desirable wild birds. At present attention is focused on primary control of bird populations by reducing the numbers of eggs hatched. Experiments with noisy deterrents have not been very successful: the birds get used to them.[8] An example of the conflict was the proposal of the US Navy to establish a $186 million outlying landing field in North Carolina near Pocosin Lakes

National Wildlife Refuge, winter home to thousands of tundra swans and snow geese. After Chesapeake Bay, it is the second most important habitat on the eastern seaboard for waterfowl. The Navy wanted to buy or condemn some 30,000 acres of property around the landing strip, intended to simulate the confined conditions of an aircraft carrier deck. It would be used for 31,000 annual practice touch-and-go landings of strike fighters. The Navy concern was BASH, bird aircraft strike hazard. One 8 kilogram (17 pound) tundra swan colliding with a 30 tonne (66,000 pound) Super Hornet strike fighter could bring down the $60 million aircraft, endangering and perhaps even killing the highly trained pilot. At the proposed site either the Navy would have to curtail training programmes in winter, when the migratory bird population was at its peak, or the refuge would have to be made less attractive for its bird residents and visitors on the Atlantic Flyway, the natural route they have used for centuries. Some 80 per cent of Atlantic Flyway tundra swans were reckoned to winter there. After more than a year's public debate, early in 2005 a federal court judge said the Navy had failed to take the required hard look at the environmental effects of the project and to consider alternatives. He halted plans to buy land and develop a runway, a decision against which the Navy appealed, unsuccessfully. The court ordered the Navy to reassess environmental impacts should the field be built, the study to be completed by early 2007.

There are many such conflicts around the world, which a volunteer organization, Bird Strike Committee USA, tries to forestall. Formed in 1991 and directed by members from the Federal Aviation Administration, the US Department of Agriculture, Department of Defense and the aviation industry, it has more than an American concern. Its annual meetings at host airports are international, with typical attendance of over 400 from more than 20 countries. In a world where over 195 people were killed as a result of bird strikes between 1988 and 2004, their aim is to understand and reduce bird and other wildlife hazards to aircraft. Bird Strike Committee USA promotes the collection, analysis and dissemination of accurate wildlife strike data. For example:

About 90% of all bird strikes in the US are by species federally protected under the Migratory Bird Treaty Act.

Waterfowl (32%), gulls (28%) and raptors (17%) represented 77% of the reported bird strikes causing damage to US civil aircraft 1990–2003.

An estimated 80% of bird strikes to US civil aircraft go unreported.

Appreciating the scale of the problem is a step to promoting the development of new technologies for reducing hazards and exchanging information on the effectiveness of wildlife control measures.

There are still plenty of individuals though who think that conservation has gone too far, that in recent decades the balance of nature has been tilted in favour of wildlife. To them the shortest answer is to treat birds as game for the hunter. To aviators and their passengers birds are 'feathered bullets', even 'missiles'. Why shouldn't they be treated in kind? Against the background of the ever-pressing need to reduce carbon emissions, the debate will continue in conferences, courts and the media.

8 Promotion

With its elegant shape and positive attributes, the swan is a natural emblem of quality. It has been used for things as diverse as inn signs, to suggest peaceful restfulness and possibly some elegance in guest houses and hotels, boats, cigarette cards, coats of arms, cruises, confectionery, cosmetics, dry cleaning, electrical appliances such as kettles and toasters, estate agents (perhaps the least deserving), fashion labels, football teams, glassware, horse brasses, insurance, lager, laundry, matches, pens and inks, software companies, swimming clubs, vapour bath essence, vehicle rental and much more. A strong bird, it builds strong brands. Even where the designation derives from the surname Swan the symbol carries more weight more readily than the name.

The swan has been represented in batik, on enamels (notably by the engravers Robert Hancock and Louis Philippe Boitard in the group of *galant* subjects in their 1751–6 Birmingham enamels that incorporated a pair of swans painted in the foreground of the compositions), in heraldry, misericords, moulds for biscuits and jellies, origami, print, screensavers on computers (including the sound of water movement), tapestries, on tombstones with angelic wings protecting the deceased, TV commercials, tiles, wallpaper. Cygnus, the carriage built in Britain between 1938 and 1951 for the Pullman Car Company, was initially reserved for use by royalty and visiting heads of state. Sculpture is a much used medium. Maurice Lambert (1901–1964) presented 'The Swan', his work in

168

The wrapper of a Russian chocolate marshmallow.

alabaster, to the Tate Gallery in 1932. It is also reproduced in fibreglass, glass, ice, metal, porcelain, stone, wood. Open at the back, it makes an elegant wine cooler.

The swan logo is the official Nordic ecolabel, introduced by the Nordic Council of Ministers representing Finland, Norway and Sweden. Covering some 60 product groups, everything from washing-up liquid to furniture and hotels, it demonstrates that a product is a good environmental choice. Throughout its lifecycle, from raw material to waste, a product's impact on the environment is assessed through tests by independent laboratories and control visits. To ensure that standards are maintained or, better, raised, criteria are revised and a label is usually valid for three years, after which a company must reapply for a licence. Consumers are encouraged to look for the swan logo.[1]

The mid-1930s trademark of the French company Helia.

English inn signs have been compulsory since a 1393 statute of Richard II, whose arms bore the White Hart. Similarly the arms of Anne of Cleves led to the increased popularity of the White Swan. The Swan Tavern at Charing Cross was fashionable in the fifteenth century, being patronized by John Howard, Duke of Norfolk. Ben Jonson once said an extempore grace before King James I, including a blessing there for Ralph, who drew him good canary, a light

The 1938 trademark of Porth Textiles, made in the coalmining Rhondda Valley, South Wales.

A mid-1950s
coffee label.

sweet wine from the Canary Islands. The Swan at Knightsbridge, the haunt of young gallants, had a bad reputation. In his 1681 play *The Soldier's Fortune* Thomas Otway has the jealous husband and father Sir David Dunce exclaim ''tis a damned house that Swan; that Swan at Knightsbridge is a confounded house!' The Swan in Exchange Alley, Cornhill, was much more respectable, the venue for concerts in the eighteenth century. In the early nineteenth century the White Swan in Vere Street, Clare Market, was a notorious homosexual brothel. The Swan in Bayswater Road, London, established in 1775, was the first stop past Tyburn gallows. When in 1676 John Wilmot, second Earl of Rochester, was involved in a riot in which a friend was killed, King Charles II ordered his arrest. Technically guilty of murder, Rochester had to go to earth, which he did at the Black Swan on Tower Hill as the 'famous Italian pathologist, Dr Alexander Bendo' in bizarre oriental dress and false beard. The great Doctor achieved fame throughout the capital. He did not practise his art solely among the artisans of East London. Patients of all ranks travelled great distances. Thus his enemies, who were painstakingly searching London for him, were themselves being palmed off with his quack remedies.[2] There was a Black Swan in York, the starting point for the four-day coach journey to the Black Swan in London.

Another busy coaching inn in the seventeenth and eighteenth centuries was The Swan with Two Necks in Lad Lane, now merged into Gresham Street in the City.[3] Often the name is thought to be a corruption of The Swan with Two Nicks, a reference to the beak mark of the Vintners' Company. That is most unlikely. Originally beak marks, scores in number, were complex designs. In 1878 they were simplified to prevent any possible suffering to the birds. The origin of the name is much earlier. Bartholomew, an English Franciscan friar who compiled his encyclopaedia *The Properties of Things*, probably before 1260, notes: 'When the swan is in love he

The Old Black Swan sign, formerly on a coaching-house in York.

seeketh the female, and pleaseth her with bedipping of the neck, and draweth her to himward; and he joineth his neck to the female's neck, as it were binding the necks together.' Henry Machyn (1498–1563), merchant tailor of London, mentions an inn sign in Milk Street in his diary for 1556. In Andrew Marvell's post-June 1667 poem 'The Loyal Scot' written 'Upon the Occasion of Captain Douglas burnt in one his Majesty's Ships at Chatham' during Charles II's first Dutch wars, are the lines

> Strange was the sight, that Scotch twin-headed man
> With single body, like the two-necked swan.

The origin may be heraldic, two birds' necks 'gorged' with a coronet.

Signs changed over the centuries, reflecting contemporary attitudes. For instance, an eighteenth-century posting house, The Swan at Fittleworth, West Sussex, on its wooden arch spanning the road featured a nude woman astride a swan. In the nineteenth century there were objections because the woman had a face uncannily like that of Queen Victoria so clothes were added to the figure. That in turn was superseded by swan portraits appropriate to the times. In the eighteenth century W. Wilson, proprietor of a posting house for the Royal Mail coach from London to Weymouth, Dorset (the Swan with Two Necks in Lad Lane mentioned above), issued trade tokens, which made up for the shortage of small change. Payable at the mail coach office in Lad Lane, the obverse featured a swan with two necks and the reverse a coach and horses with the motto Speed, Regularity and Security.[4] A swan penny of similar date payable in Middlesex had a swan swimming on the obverse.[5] The Swan by London Bridge, which gave its name to Swan Stairs, issued trade tokens as early as 1657. With a representation of a swan walking on Old London Bridge, they made the point that it was the Swan above

Swan signs occur frequently in Western Australia; the Cricket Association is just one example.

The traditional pose emphasizes the quality of a Norwich jeweller.

Not all pub swan signs have the bird in a traditional stately pose. This water-skiing bird can be seen in Sherborne, Dorset.

the Bridge against the Swan below, the one at Dowgate. Samuel Pepys dined there in 1660 and was unimpressed. A combination on trade tokens is the Swan and Sugarloaf, the latter coming from a grocer's sign. Other combinations include Swan and Antelope, Bottle, Cygnets, Falcon, Harlequin, Helmet, Hoop, Horseshoe, Rummer (a large drinking glass) and Salmon. An existing inn with a new licence was The Swan Revived. The Swan's Nest, Swan in Rushes and Three Cygnets speak for themselves.[6]

The bird appeared not just in mediaeval heraldry but also in modern seals and coats of arms. For instance, in the railway building boom of the 1840s it was adopted on the seals of four Buckinghamshire railway companies: Buckinghamshire; Buckingham & Brackley; Oxford & Bletchley; Watford & Edgware. The swan was taken from one of the badges of the Staffords, first Dukes of Buckingham. It was also adopted by the Borough of Buckingham and the County of Buckinghamshire. The coat of arms for Buckinghamshire, granted in 1948, features a white swan

In the British railway boom beginning in 1830 heraldic swans appeared in a number of railway company seals. In Buckinghamshire the swan was taken from one of the badges of the Staffords, Dukes of Buckingham.

in chains, the link to the king, a reference to the period when the birds were bred locally for the king's pleasure. The arms are supported on the sinister side by a swan rousant an emblem of the River Thames.[7] Other towns in the county recognize the association with the bird. Marlow's coat of arms, granted in 1989, has a swan on the crest, the chain removed to indicate the freedom of the town, and a foot resting on a gold hub with a blue flash of lightning representing the modern industries there.[8] High Wycombe has a Swan Theatre.

Towards the end of the twentieth century, by popular vote, Finland chose six nature symbols to draw attention to the country's wildlife and promote appreciation of it. Of the six the swan has taken on the strongest symbolic value. In the west of Finland the whooper swan was considered a game bird, in the east sacred. By the 1950s it was almost extinct, about ten nesting pairs surviving in the remote north and east. One man, Yrjö Kokko, a vet in Lapland, ensured the survival of the species by documenting its life in a book *The Whooper Swan* (1950), which raised public awareness, reinforced by a second book *They Are Returning* (1954). The bird was made a protected species and in the twenty-first century there are some 2,000 nesting pairs spread throughout the country. They are backed by ancient traditions as seen in the rock drawings, for instance of a swan with an egg, of the reindeer-herding Sámi people at Lake Onega, dating from about 2,000 BCE. They are also heard in Sibelius's often performed symphonic poem *Swan of Tuonela*. A white swan in flight silhouetted against a blue sky looks like the reverse of the national flag, the blue cross against a field of white.

Another symbol of place is the swan boats of Boston, Massachusetts. Harbingers of spring, they have appeared on the Public Garden Lagoon since 1877, when Robert Paget was granted a boat for hire licence by the city. He capitalized on the bicycle principle with the help of others and developed a catamaran housing a paddle wheel arrangement that was foot propelled. To cover the captain he suggested a swan, an idea that came to him from his love of Wagner's opera *Lohengrin*. Initially the boats were single-seaters carrying eight passengers, a number that has risen to twenty in the modern replicas.[9] They feature in E. B. White's children's story *The Trumpet of the Swan* (1970), in which trumpeter swan Louis learns to speak to the world with a trumpet stolen from a music store by

In the centre of Boston Public Garden, the oldest botanical garden in the USA, people pedal flat-bottomed boats around the artificial pond.

his father. Helped by a boy named Sam, Louis learns how to read and write. This make-believe world was animated in 2001. Similar boats are to be seen at other leisure sites, for instance Disneyland Paris, Thorpe Park in the UK, on the River Douro in Portugal and in Prague on the Vltava River. Up in the Central Highlands of Vietnam, in the Annamese Mountain range, one of the kitsch attractions for honeymooners at Dalat in the Valley of Love is the swan-shaped paddleboats on Xuang Huong Lake.

A tourist attraction involving performing birds is the moat to the palace of the Bishop of Bath and Wells, near Wells Cathedral in Somerset. The daughter of Bishop Hervey (1869–1894) trained the swans to ring a bell when they wanted feeding. Their skill fell into disuse until their descendants were trained once more in about 1969, to the delight of visitors.[10]

In 1883 Collard & Company of Liverpool began manufacturing Swan Vestas, the matchbox depicting a swan on a pond with rushes and water lilies in the background. The product had a

Generations of swans in the moat of the Bishop's Palace at Wells, Somerset, have inherited the technique of ringing the bell for food, which is thrown from the window.

BRYANT & MAY'S
SWAN VESTAS.

The Ideal Match for Smokers.

Designs of Swan Vesta matchboxes have been updated periodically, to the delight of phillumenists.

No. 12 Box.

SUPPORT HOME INDUSTRIES
THE SWAN TRADE MARK
REG NO 234938.
WHITE PINE VESTAS
MADE ONLY BY BRYANT & MAY Ltd
LONDON & LIVERPOOL

respectable ancestry. Vesta was the Roman goddess of the hearth, worshipped in every household and in a temple in the Roman forum that held a fire said to have been brought from Troy and attended by Vestal Virgins. The fire was never allowed to go out. Every town had its temple of Vesta, an ancient symbol of fire as the source of life. Swan Vesta was not the first use of Vesta applied to a match. In her 1839 children's novel, a deliberate antithesis of the contemporary moralizing tales for the young, the Scottish writer Catherine Sinclair (1800–1864) wrote: 'Laura afterwards singed a hole in her muslin frock while lighting one of the Vesta matches.' The name Swan, of course, capitalized on all the virtuous attributes of the bird. It was a good example of branding a basic product, giving something mundane a distinct identity. By the Edwardian period, when it was promoted as 'the smoker's match', users simply asked for a box of Swans. Other matches lacked an identity. Users included royalty and Swan as a quality image was reinforced by having the Royal Warrant. The brand

'Be clean in everything that concerns your baby'. A 1939 Works Progress Administration poster by Erik Hans Krause, using a swan and cygnet to promote cleanliness and proper care of American children.

had international significance. It was exported within the Empire and to the United States as a safety match.

During the First World War the Knapsack Box, a metal container with a spring lid, was popular with troops. On the home market between 1914 and 1917 the company offered a free accident life assurance policy on condition that travellers were carrying a box of Swan Vestas at the time of the accident. In line with the fashion for women smoking, Dainty Swan Vestas ('For My Lady') were marketed between 1920 and 1933. The image was carried over into objects such as aprons, ashtrays, dartboards, key rings, knives, map cases, pens, playing cards and postcards. All over Britain the company sold seaside postcards with two attractive young ladies pictured above the matchbox and an individual resort name, e.g. 'Some striking things in "Matchless" Littlehampton'. Holidaymakers sending greetings to friends and relatives thus paid to advertise the product. By the 1930s Swans had become Britain's bestselling match, accounting for half the turnover of the owner, Bryant & May, which had acquired the original manufacturer. So successful was the brand that early in the Second World War the company bought a Spitfire for the Royal Air Force. Naturally it was named The Swan.

To follow trends, although essentially the image has remained the same, over the years various designs and colours of matchbox were produced. They have become collectors' items among phillumenists. *Vesta* was the title given to a monthly magazine for matchbox label collectors. In the mid-1980s Bryant & May, soon to become a wholly owned subsidiary of the Swedish Match Company, carried over the swan label when introducing papers for rolling one's own cigarettes. The content was Swan tobacco.[11] Although the use of matches has declined in competition with lighters, the brand survives both as a match and a lighter, as well as a cigarette filter.

Not all swan promotions are a success. Trying to capitalize on her celebrity status, in 1996 supermodel Naomi Campbell 'wrote'

Between the two world wars Japanese products had the reputation of being cheap copies of western goods. This matchbox relied on the swan image for an impression of quality.

a novel, *Swan.* When it flopped she admitted that her only role as an 'author' had been to dictate her thoughts into a tape recorder, leaving her editor Caroline Upcher to flesh them out. It was a ghostwriting failure. In 1990s slang swan became a term for the amphetamine most commonly known as Ecstasy. The term derives from the picture of a swan stamped on some of the tablets.[12]

These though are exceptions. Overall the swan is a bird to be admired. Indeed, it makes the perfect present. In the UK you need a licence to own mute swans, a bureaucratic process which can take months to arrange, but you can buy black swans. A magazine such as *Game Bird and Conservationists' Gazette* will give advice to prospective purchasers on where to go. For the person who has everything the birds are an elegant sight and an unusual talking point, an ideal addition to the lake at their country house. The only trouble is that they carry no guarantee to remain there. Unless pinioned, they might migrate to a neighbour's lake.

For most people the swan is a desirable bird, a beautiful ornament worth protecting, legally or in recognised wetlands. Natural habitats and swan sanctuaries attract continuing and determined support. The conservation movement is international. It outweighs the fragmented opposition. The swan earns its respect on its merits, not out of pity or sentimentality easily bestowed on the plight of some wildlife. Everything seems to be going for it. What can possibly go wrong?

The lurking fear is an avian flu pandemic, spread over distances by migrating swans, that could entail the culling of thousands of birds. For all our sakes we must hope it does not happen.

ПУДРА
„ЛЕБЯЖІЙ ПУХЪ„

ИЗОБРѢТЕНІЕ

Т_{ВА} БРОКАРЪ и К^о

МОСКВА.

Timeline of the Swan

c. 80 million BCE	*c.* 1.8 million BCE	*c.* 4,500 BCE	2nd millennium BCE
Descended from dinosaurs, members of the swan family already existed by this time	The giant swan of Malta	Mesolithic animal sculptures in Southern Scandinavia	The swan was a cult bird in the European Bronze Ag

1804	1806	1812–22
Thomas Bewick's *Water Birds* published	Whistling (tundra) swan discovered in western USA	Brothers Grimm publish folklore

1883	1891	1946	1950	1968
Swan Vesta matches introduced	Society for the Protection of Birds founded UK	Peter Scott founds The Wildlife Trust in UK	Nature Conservancy founded in USA	Trumpeter Swan Society founded in USA

| 1st millennium BCE | Middle Ages | 1697 | 1801 |

Classical myths, e.g. Leda and the Swan, written down

Folklore of swan maidens and swan knights

Europeans first hear of a black swan in Western Australia

Thomas Young expounds wave theory of light, based on observations of ripples made by swans

| 1827–35 | 1850 | 1877 |

Audubon's *The Birds of America*

Hans Christian Andersen's *The Ugly Duckling*

Wagner's *Lohengrin* (Knight of the Swan)

Tchaikovsky's *Swan Lake*

| 1971 | 1991 | 2002 | 2004 |

International convention on saving wetlands signed at Ramsar, Iran. Anglers' lead weights banned in UK

Non-toxic shot required for waterfowl hunting in USA (1999 Canada)

British list of bird species reclassified by DNA, putting mute swan at head of list, closest to prehistoric ancestors

Bird flu virus kills ten black swans in Shenzen Zoo, southern China

References

1 CLAMOROUS WINGS

1 Alan G. Knox *et al.*, 'Taxonomic Recommendations for British Birds', *Ibis*, CXLIV/4, pp. 707–10.

2 Peter Richards, ed., *Cambridge Encyclopaedia of Ornithology* (Cambridge, 1991),p. 11.

3 Ibid., p. 62.

4 Paul Valéry, *Variété III* (Paris, 1936), p. 217.

5 Thomas Hood, *Miss Kilmansegg: Her Honeymoon*, l. 1852, *Stevenson's Book of Quotations* (London, 1974), p. 1949.

6 Letter to the Countess of Upper Ossory, 1 December 1786, *Oxford Dictionary of Quotations* (Oxford, 1979).

7 T.H.D. Mahoney, *Edmund Burke and Ireland* (Harvard, 1960), p. 30.

8 In John A. Chapple and Arthur Pollard, eds, *The Letters of Mrs Gaskell* (Manchester, 1966), p. 305.

9 Desmond Morris, *Animal Watching* (London, 1990), p. 206.

10 Norman MacCaig, 'Intruder in a Set Scene', in *Collected Poems* (London, 1985).

11 William Shakespeare, *Henry VI, Part 1*, v.iii.56.

12 P. Bateson *et al.*, 'Similarities between the Faces of Parents and Offspring in Bewick's Swan and the Differences between Mates', *Journal of the Zoological Society of London*, CXCI (1980), pp. 61–74.

13 Ivan G. Sparkes, *Dictionary of Collective Nouns and Group Terms* (London, 1975), p. 177; Rex Collings, *A Crash of Rhinoceroses* (London, 1992), pp. 151 and 163.

14 John Dryden, trans., *Aeneid*, VII, 965.

15 Peter Richards, ed., *Cambridge Encyclopaedia of Ornithology* (Cambridge, 1991), p. 14.

16 *Daily Mail*, 26 May 2004, p. 3.

17 Peter Hayman and Philip Burton, *The Bird Life of Britain* (London, 1976) p. 223.

18 In Valerie Grove, *Laurie Lee* (London, 1999), p. 199.

19 Sir Philip Sidney, Sonnet 54, *Astrophil and Stella*, in *Selected Writings* (Manchester, 1987), p. 55.

20 Christopher Lever, *They Dined on Eland* (London, 1992), pp. 110, 127, 142, 144.

21 Ibid., pp. 76, 136, 138, 144, 151, 156.

22 Juvenal, *Satires*, VI, 165.

23 John Wesley, *Journal*, 2 October 1764.

24 James A. Powell *et al.*, 'Optimal Trajectory for the Short-Distance Foraging Flights of Swans', *Journal of Theoretical Biology*, CCIV/3 (2000), pp. 415–30.

2 GRACE AND FAVOUR

1 In Duff Hart-Davis, *Audubon's Elephant* (London, 2003), p. 115.

2 Henry James, *Confidence* (New York, 1962), p. 111.

3 Rosamond Lehmann, *The Ballad and the Source* (London, 1982), p. 231.

4 *The Times*, 17 November 2003, p. 27.

5 William Wordsworth, *The Prelude*, I , l. 376.

6 John Milton, *Paradise Lost*, VII, l. 438.

7 In Orlando Figes, *Natasha's Dance* (London, 2003), pp. 533–4.

8 James Elroy Flecker, 'The Old Ships', *An Anthology of Modern Verse* (London, 1921), p. 15.

9 P. B. Shelley, *Prometheus Unbound*, II, v, 72–4.

10 William Shakespeare, *As You Like It*, I.iii.72.

11 Lucretius, *De Rerum Natura*, IV, l. 181.

12 Virgil, *Eclogues*, IX, 32.

13 Edmund Spenser, *Shephearde's Calendar*, October, l. 89, in *Poetical Works* (Oxford, 1963).

14 Jean de La Fontaine, 'Le Cygne et le cuisinier', in *Fables*, trans. Marianne Moore (New York, 1954), p. 68.

15 Aesop, *Fables* (London, 1954), p. 84.

16 Plato, *Phaedo*, 84e.

17 Sir Edward Coke, *Decision*, Case of the Swans, 4 *Rep.* 85, quoting Martial, *Epigrams*, Bk XIII, epig. 77.

18 William Shakespeare, *Rape of Lucrece*, l. 1611.

19 William Shakespeare, *Othello*, v.ii.245.

20 William Shakespeare, *Merchant of Venice*, III.ii.44.

21 Alfred, Lord Tennyson, 'The Passing of Arthur', l. 434, in *Idylls of the King*, ed. J. M. Gray (Harmondsworth, 1973).

22 Samuel Coleridge, 'Epigram on a Volunteer Singer', *Oxford Dictionary of Quotations* (Oxford, 1979).

23 Mark Twain, *Speeches* (New York, 1923), p. 255.

24 John Stuart Mill, *A System of Logic*, 9th edn (London, 1875), vol. I, bk 3, ch. 3, para. 2.

25 *Bestiary: Being an English Version of MS Bodley 764*, trans. Richard Barber (London, 1992).

26 Diana Souhami, *Wild Girls: Paris, Sappho and Art* (London, 2004), p. 13.

27 Ibid., p. 57.

28 Ben Jonson, *Volpone*, I.v.110.

29 Geraldine Cummins, *Swan on a Black Sea* (London, 1965).

30 Rosamund Lehmann, *The Swan in the Evening* (London, 1967), pp. 45–6.

3 TRANSFORMATIONS

1 Maeve Binchy, in the *Oxford Dictionary of Literary Quotations*, p. 170.

2 Ovid, *Metamorphoses*, bk II, 373–80, trans. Frank Miller, rev. G. P. Goold (London, 1916).

3 Robert Harris, *Hannibal*, chap. 97, para. 2.

4 www.janenevillegallery.co.uk/hannibal.html

5 Sir James Frazer, *The Golden Bough* (London, 1936), vol. I, p. 200.

1 *Encyclopaedia Britannica Online*, 'Measurement systems'.
2 Ibid., 'Figureheads, Rome'.
3 Ibid., 'Furniture'.
4 A. H. Smith, *The Place Names of the East Riding of Yorkshire* (Cambridge, 1937), p. 219.
5 In John Richardson, *Annals of London* (London, 2000), p. 101.
6 In Ben Weinreb and Christopher Hibbert, eds, *The London Encyclopaedia* (London, 1993), p. 874.
7 In John Dover Wilson, *Life in Shakespeare's England* (London, 1949), p. 17.
8 www.selbyabbey.org.uk/history.htm (accessed 29 March 2007).
9 Dorothy Margaret Stuart, *A Book of Birds and Beasts* (London, 1957), pp. 20–21.
10 www.trabel.com/brugge/bruges-minnewater (accessed 12 August 2007).
11 Erwin Weber, *The Lutheran Journal*, LXV/2 (1996).
12 Marc Alexander, *A Companion to the Folklore, Myths and Customs of Britain* (Stroud, 2002), p. 282.
13 Oliver St John Gogarty, *An Offering of Swans* (Dublin, 1923), Preface.
14 Helen F. Boehm, *With a Little Luck . . .* (New York, 1985), pp. 120–21.
15 In Ted Morgan, *Somerset Maugham* (London, 1980), p. 392.
16 Valerie Grove, *Laurie Lee* (London, 1999), p. 262.
17 In Jenny Uglow, *The Lunar Men* (London, 2002), p. 127.
18 *New Grove Dictionary of Music* (London, 1980), vol. 17, p. 281.
19 Ibid., vol. 16, p. 402.
20 *All Music Guide to Rock*, ed. Chris Woodstra (San Francisco, 1997), p. 1163.
21 In George Peacock, *Life of Thomas Young* (London, 1855), pp. 142–3.

5 HAZARDS

1 Henning Mankell, *Before the Frost* (London, 2004), p. 12.
2 Daniel Defoe, *Robinson Crusoe* (London, 1985), p. 176.

3 Jules Verne, *Around the World in 80 Days*, trans. George M. Towle (Project Gutenberg, 1994) chap. 1.

4 Georgina O'Hara, *The Encyclopaedia of Fashion* (London, 1989), p. 108.

5 Stephen Greenblatt, *Will in the World* (London, 2004), p. 172.

6 Gustave Flaubert, *Madame Bovary* (1857), trans. Alan Russell (London, 1950), p. 276.

7 Cyril Pearl, *The Girl with the Swansdown Seat* (London, 1955).

8 Henry Longfellow, *The Song of Hiawatha* – 11, *Hiawatha's Wedding Feast*, (London, 1908).

9 In *The Times* and *Daily Mail*, 19 March 2005, p. 7.

6 FOOD

1 *Leviticus*, 11, 18.

2 *Deuteronomy*, 14, 16.

3 Robert May, *The Accomplisht Cook* (London, 1678), p. 458.

4 Harleian MS 4016.

5 MS Ashmole 1439.

6 Alan Davidson, *The Oxford Companion to Food* (Oxford, 1999), p. 772.

7 Orlando Figes, *Natasha's Dance* (London, 2003), p. 164.

8 Matthew Prior, *Alma* (1717), 1, 379.

9 C. B. Jewson, *History of the Great Hospital Norwich* (Norwich, 1966).

10 *Mrs Beeton's All About Cookery* (London, 1923), p. 569.

11 *Oxford Dictionary of National Biography* (Oxford, 2004), W. E. Gladstone.

12 Ibid., Jo Bertorelli.

7 CONSERVATION

1 Christina Hole, *A Dictionary of British Folk Customs* (Oxford, 1976), pp. 287–9; www.thamesweb.co.uk/swans/upping2 (accessed 29 March 2007).

2 *Swan Marking and Swan Upping*, The Dyers' Company (London,

2000); *The Vintners' Swans,* The Vintners' Company (London, n.d.).

3 www.challenger.ca/trumpeter_swans (accessed 13 August 2007).

4 *Daily Telegraph*, obituary, 14 June 2003.

5 Tom Fort, 'The Case for Killing Swans', *Spectator*, 12 June 2004.

6 www.dnr.state.md.us/wildlife/msmpcomments (accessed 13 August 2007).

7 *Wildlife Hazards to Aviation*, ICAO/ACI Airports Conference, Miami, Florida, 24 April 2001.

8 'Bird-Strike Solutions Spurred by Imagination, Innovation', *Flight Safety Foundation Airport Operations*, XXI/2 (March–April 1995); *Large Flocking Birds* (CAP721), Safety Regulation Group, Civil Aviation Authority.

8 PROMOTION

1 www.svanen.nu/Eng/about (accessed 29 March 2007).

2 Cephas Goldsworthy, *The Satyr* (London, 2001), p. 203.

3 Mary Cathcart Borer, *The City of London* (London, 1977), p. 247.

4 Peter Mathias, *English Trade Tokens* (London, 1962), pp. 40–41.

5 R. Dalton and S. H. Hamer, *The Provincial Token-Coinage of the Eighteenth Century* (Lawrence, MA, 1977).

6 J. Larwood, *English Inn Signs* (London, 1985), pp. 136–9.

7 www.civicheraldry.co.uk/bucks (accessed 13 August 2007).

8 *The Marlow Historian*, II (2002), pp. 3–6.

9 www.swanboats.com (accessed 29 March 2007).

10 Maria Jepps, *Wells, A History and Celebration* (London, 2004).

11 J. H. Luker, *Swan Centenary 1883–1983* (Vesta Publications, 1983).

12 Jonathon Green, *Dictionary of Slang* (London, 1999), p. 1163.

Bibliography

Beaver, Patrick, *The Matchmakers* (London, 1985)

Birkhead, Mike and Christopher Perrins, *The Mute Swan* (London, 1986)

Brown Michelle P., and Patricia Lovett, *The Historical Source Book for Scribes* (London, 1999)

Buczacki, Stefan, *Fauna Britannica* (London, 2002)

Collins Pocket Guide, Stars & Planets (London, 1993)

Cooper, J. C., *An Illustrated Encyclopaedia of Traditional Symbols* (London, 1979)

——, *Brewer's Myth and Legend* (London, 1992)

Crisp, Tony, *The New Dream Dictionary* (London, 1994)

Dorer, Lis, *Swans in my Kitchen* (Dunstable, 1995)

Fox-Davies, Arthur Charles, *A Complete Guide to Heraldry* (London, 1993)

Gloag, John, *A Short Dictionary of Furniture* (London, 1969)

Gordon, Stuart, *The Encyclopaedia of Myths and Legends* (London, 1993)

Goulden, Sally L., *Diseases in the Mute Swan*, National Swan Sanctuary

Heraldry Sources, Symbols and Meaning (London, 1997)

Jones, Alison, *Dictionary of World Folklore* (London, 1995)

Miller, Judith, *The Illustrated Dictionary of Antiques & Collectables* (London, 2001)

——, *Miller's Antiques Encyclopaedia* (London, 1998)

Ogilvie, Malcolm and Steve Young, *Wildfowl of the World* (London, 2002)

The Penguin Dictionary of Symbols (London, 1996)

Rees, Alwyn and Brinley, *Celtic Heritage* (London, 1961)

Richardson, Joanna, *Baudelaire* (London, 1994)

Savage, George, and Harold Newman, *An Illustrated Dictionary of Ceramics* (London, 1976)

Scott, Peter and The Wildfowl Trust, *The Swans* (London, 1972)

Smith, Al, *Dictionary of City of London Street Names* (Newton Abbot, 1970)

Spencer, Colin, *British Food* (London, 2002)

Swann, H. K., *A Dictionary of English and Folk-Names of British Birds* (Wakefield, 1977)

Ticehurst, N. F., *The Mute Swan in England* (London, 1957)

Wernham, Chris *et al.*, *The Migration Atlas, Movements of the Birds of Britain and Ireland* (London, 2002)

Wilson, C. Anne, *Food and Drink in Britain* (London, 1973)

Young, Steve, *An Essential Guide to Bird Photography* (Lewes, 2001)

——, *A Field Guide to Bird Photography* (Lewes, 2002)

Associations and Websites

There are many regional and local societies devoted to bird watching, natural history, ornithology, swan rescue and preservation. Examples are The Maryland Ornithological Society, based in Baltimore, and the Rongcheng Whooper Swan Protection Association in Shandong Province, East China.

National organizations often have offices and sites where there is a population of specific birds. Some of the better-known international and national bodies include:

BIRDLIFE INTERNATIONAL
A global partnership having regional offices in Africa, Americas, Asia, Europe and the Middle East.
Wellbrook Court, Girton Road, Cambridge, CB3 0NA, UK

BIRDS AUSTRALIA
www.birdsaustralia.com.au

BIRD STUDIES CANADA
www.bsc-eoc.org

BIRDWATCH IRELAND
bird@indigo.ie

BRITISH TRUST FOR ORNITHOLOGY
www.bto.org

CANADIAN NATURE FEDERATION
www.cnf.ca

ENGLISH NATURE
www.english-nature.org.uk

NATIONAL AUDUBON SOCIETY
700 Broadway, New York, NY 10003, USA

THE ROYAL FOREST AND BIRD PROTECTION SOCIETY
forestandbird.org.nz
172 Taranaki Street, PO Box 631, Wellington, New Zealand

ROYAL SOCIETY FOR THE PROTECTION OF BIRDS
www.rspb.org.uk
The Lodge, Sandy, Bedfordshire, SG19 2DL, UK

THE SWAN SANCTUARY
swans@swanuk.org.uk
Felix Lane, Shepperton, Middlesex, TW17 8NN, UK

THE TRUMPETER SWAN SOCIETY
12615 County Road 9, Suite #100, Plymouth, Minnesota 55441-1248,
USA

WILD BIRD SOCIETY OF JAPAN
www.wbsj.org
1/F Odakyu Nishi Shinjuku Building, 1-47-1 Hatsudai Shibuya-ku,
Tokyo 151-061, Japan

THE WILDLIFE & WETLANDS TRUST
www.wwt.org.uk
Slimbridge, Gloucestershire, GL2 7BT, UK

Acknowledgements

I am grateful for the help I have received in the course of researching and writing *Swan*. Particular individuals I would like to thank are Kath Baldwin, Jean Bates, Dr Sarah Bendall, Marion Boughton, Malcolm Butler, Headley and Mary Caryer, Hilda Clancy-Mulvenna, Wilfred Court, Ivan Crowe, Bob and Celia deVekey, Len Dixon, Vernon Harding, Bob Harrap, Margaret Hollowell, Anita Hooper, Anna Johnston, Philip Knights, Georgina Kynaston, Mark L'Argent, Lawrence Long, Patricia Lovett, Dr John Markham, Helena Martinova, Douglas Matthews, Derek Meakings, Flemming Møller, Chris Mullen, Lynn Palmer, Hugh Parrott, David Robertson, Baron Rochard, Terry Quinn, Bobby Reynolds, Anne Shingleton, David Souden, William Spencer, Suzanne Starbucks, Judy and Trevor Stokes, Pat Tucker, Michael Venus, Dr Lesley Walton, Deryck Weatherall, Ed Welfare, David Wheeler, Simon Young, Stephanie Zarach.

Among the institutions that have been helpful are Abbotsbury Swannery; Airfield Wildlife Management Ltd; BBC Natural History Library; British Trust for Ornithology; Castle Museum, York; Cambridge, Crawley and Croydon public libraries; Culture Archive, Brighton; the Dyers' Company; EDF Energy; Emmanuel College, Cambridge; Esperanto Museum, Gray, Haute-Saone; Gonville and Caius College, Cambridge; Great Hospital, Norwich; Historia; Japanese Embassy, London; Marlow Town Council, Buckinghamshire; National Railway Museum, York; National Swan Sanctuary; Norfolk Record Office; Polish Cultural Institute; Secret World Wildlife Rescue; Spelthorne Borough Council, Staines; the Swedish Match Co.; university libraries of Cambridge, Kent and Sussex; the Vintners' Company.

Photo Acknowledgements

The author and publishers wish to express their thanks to the following sources of illustrative material and/or permission to use it. Locations, etc., of some items are also given below.

Alte Pinakothek, Munich: p. 144; courtesy of the author: p. 116; photo Kath Baldwin: p. 26 (top); photos Jean Bates: pp. 14, 28, 104, 171, 172 (right), 173; photo courtesy Bonhams: p. 48; photo Ian Brennan: p. 42; British Museum, London: p. 93; photos courtesy of Canes Through The Ages: p. 47; photos Culture Archive pp. 50, 169 (middle and foot), 170, 179; photos courtesy of the artist (Ian Davie): p. 133; photo Ivan Day: p. 149 (foot); photo © Anna Dzondzua/2007 iStock International Inc.: p. 156; Gemäldegalerie, Berlin: pp. 68, 73; Goethe-Museum, Frankfurt-am-Main: p. 43; courtesy of the Great Hospital, Norwich: pp. 141, 142, 149 (top); Gustave Moreau Museum, Paris: p. 76; photos Margaret Hollowell pp. 26 (foot), 89, 90, 95, 172 (left); photo courtesy of Georgina Kynaston: p. 37; photos Library of Congress, Washington, DC (Prints and Photographs Division): pp. 41 (LC-USZ62-94047), 114 (LC-USZC4-10063), 157 (LC-DIG-pga-00476), 160 foot (LC-DIG-ppmsc-05086); Library of Congress (Work Projects Administration Poster Collection): p. 178 (LC-USZC2-938); Mauritshuis, The Hague: p. 145; photo Derek Meakings: p. 175; photo National Railway Museum, York: p. 174; photo courtesy of Dreweatt Neale: p. 35; photo © Dainel Olson/2007 iStock International Inc.: p. 6; Agnes Miller Parker/Culture Archive: p. 50; photo Pennsylvania Game Commission/Hal Korber: p. 25 (foot); Rex Features: pp. 22 (Rex Features, 569065L), 23 (Rex

Index